[Altar]ed Culture

Discovering the Path to a Culture of Worship

By Eric L. Freeman

Endorsements

There is nothing more important for the church to learn than how to define and practice a lifestyle of worship. Worship is so much more than a song, a service, a performance or an event. After ten years of being Eric's pastor, friend and co-worship leader I know he understands this, he is a worshipper. This book will empower you to grow as a worshiper and begin creating a culture of worship in your life, marriage, family and ministry team.

Dr. Allen Holmes
Lead Pastor
Daystar Church

One of the things I love most about Eric is the extraordinary consistency in his life. These powerful insights into an "altared life" of worship aren't a re-hash of pop church culture. Instead, they flow out of a vital, passionate pursuit of God—and they will ignite fresh fire in your pursuit too. No one is too early or too advanced in their spiritual journey to glean transformative truths and applications from this fresh work!

Jerome Daley, Leadership Coach & Culture Consultant, author of six books at www.iThrive9.com

Eric Freeman is not just an accomplished musician and gifted leader, but a talented writer who communicates the heart of worship with Scriptural insight and story-telling that reveals he is, at his core, a Worship Pastor. We need more Worship Leaders like him!

Pastor Ross Parsley
ONEchapel

In today's worship movement, much of the focus is placed on the art of music rather than the culture of worship. Eric Freeman explores what it means to discover and establish a worship community that transcends the styles and trends of worship music. This book will challenge anyone leading worship in the local church to look deeper into the heart of their worship community.

John Larson
Worship Pastor
Church of the Highlands

Eric Freeman has given his life to serve the local church. What he writes in here has come out of not only a passion for worship but a faithfulness to serve the people of God. I am grateful for him and am confident you will be encouraged and challenged by what he has written.

Glenn Packiam
Associate Pastor, New Life Church and author of Lucky, Secondhand Jesus and Butterfly in Brazil

Contents

Dedication

Foreword — 8

Section 1: The Culture that Jesus Lived

    Chapter 1 - The Uncharted Journey — 13

    Chapter 2 - Where You Go, I Go — 22

    Chapter 3 - Water, Water, Everywhere… But Not a Drop to Drink — 30

    Chapter 4 - It's the Beginning of Wisdom — 42

Section 2: First Steps

    Chapter 5 - The Path to Intimacy — 54

    Chapter 6 - The Secret Whisperer — 67

Section 3: The Path to a New Culture

    Chapter 7 - Milepost 1: Let Go, Let Loose — 82

    Chapter 8 - Milepost 2: The Anchor of Identity — 93

    Chapter 9 - Milepost 3: Childhood Fantasies — 106

    Chapter 10 - Milepost 4: Choose What Is Best — 117

    Chapter 11 - Milepost 5: Altaring Moments — 132

Section 4: Our Culture Destination

    Chapter 12 - Creating Culture — 147

    Chapter 13 - Leading Tribal Worship — 161

About The Author — 172

Acknowledgements — 173

NOTES — 174

© Copyright 2012 Eric Freeman

All rights reserved. No portion of this book may be reproduced, stored in a retrieval system, or transmitted in any form or by any means-electronic, mechanical, photocopy, recording, or other-except for brief quotations in printed reviews, without the prior written permission of the author.

All Scripture quotations, unless otherwise noted, are taken from the *Holy Bible, English Standard Version®. ESV®*. Copyright ©2003 Crossway Bibles, a division of Good News Publishers. All rights reserved. NLT quotations are taken from the *Holy Bible, New Living Translation*, copyright ©1996 Tyndale House Publishers, Inc. All rights reserved. NKJV quotations are taken from the New King James Version, copyright ©1982 Thomas Nelson, Inc. All rights reserved. MSG quotations are taken from *THE MESSAGE*, copyright ©1993 Eugene H. Peterson, NavPress Publishing Group.

Dedication

To each person that comprises the Body of Christ at Daystar Church.

Partnering together to do whatever it takes to make Christ followers who Grow, Connect, Serve, and Partner together!

Foreword

The subject of worship culture can be an overwhelming topic at first glance. How do we create such a thing or measure it once it's created? The signs of a healthy worship environment can be so subjective and the methods don't always translate from place to place. What looks effective on a grand scale can come across pretentious in a more basic setting. On the other hand, frustration can easily set in when what seems deeply good and right to us doesn't always grow to be big. To get our bearing in this conundrum, Eric Freeman helps us focus more on the underlying themes that transfer well as a set of lived beliefs—values that form us, language that shapes our communication, and actions that reveal our true identity.

I often try to compare matters in the church to the household dynamics in a family. My wife and I have four children—two boys, two girls. They have different personalities. They are at different stages of development. And my wife and I are very different as well. Though we have various parts to us, and sometimes contradicting elements, there is a cohesion that pulls us together as a tight community. The marks of cohesion in a great family are the same indicators for a great church. The job of leaders, parents, and participants alike must involve receiving, transferring, and contributing to this cohesion.

First, spiritual formation and the instilling of character takes place in a **personal** environment. Jesus spoke to the masses, but He called his disciples by name. The Bible cannot make a Christian; that only happens in a personal interaction with God. Our teachings, services, and programs do not produce health or wholeness; they merely set the table for individuals to commune with God and one another. The role of worship ministry is like the role of the phone company: We connect two parties. But we cannot connect people to something we ourselves are not connected to. We must know and be known. In a place where personal relationships are shallow, worship culture quickly runs dry.

Out of personal relationships comes healthy **resistance**. Roles, function, and performance should never eclipse the evolution of identity and belief. This clash is most obvious in a college setting. There's a magic that takes place when a bunch of fresh, sapling children-with-adult-bodies park themselves under the tutelage of mature, stable oaks of wisdom. Sparks fly when ideas collide. It's a recipe for fireworks...and for growth. Love and hate. Always drama.

All of us who care deeply about the local church love this drama and long to capture the fireworks that typically ignite during the university years and make them burn for a lifetime. The family of faith is ultimately a culture of worship that contains large spectrum of people. It can be the sandbox for the young, the training gym of the adolescent, and the refinery of the wise.

Finally, once personal commitment engages with dramatic resistance—a **communal death and life**—a synergy takes place that becomes an aroma of Christ. 2 Corinthians 2:16 says, "To the one we are the smell of death; to the other, the fragrance of life." Our churches become like the temple of the Old Testament where sacrifices are offered, cleansing from sin takes place, and the radiance of His presence fills the people.

Church. Family. Life. God. These are not meant to be overly safe environments. Holiness is a messy business. There is no arrival at cultural utopia, only a deeper journey in favor with God and man.

How do we integrate this habitual holiness into our current communal struggle for establishment-of-self and dominance over environment? This book wrestles with these questions and offers a fresh posture toward them. Eric Freeman is a relentless pilgrim, seeking to build up the body of Christ into maturity. His message is timeless, and is ears are tuned to the wind of the Spirit. His prayer, as well as mine, is that we continue in the faith that Jesus offers and the life that only he gives, that we shed the ways of man and the snares of sin, so we might share in the suffering and resurrection of our glorious Father.

Jared Anderson

Section 1
The Culture that Jesus Lived

Chapter 1

The Uncharted Journey

It all began with a dream. A dream so large that if obtained, my life would never be the same. Whether I wanted to admit it or not, I was consumed. I was walking the path I had chosen for my life with determination and, perhaps, desperation. My course was set, my eyes focused, and I anxiously awaited the next step toward my dream. "What is this dream?" you may ask... That is a great question. Let's start from the beginning.

From an early age I was fascinated with cars, engines, and the whole experience of going fast. My dream was to become a motor-sports engineer. I wanted to design and build engines for NASCAR. I loved the power, the sounds, and the intricacies of the motor. I was fascinated with the challenge of making it faster and more efficient. I guess it comes down to the fact that I love speed.

I often tell my wife that I think God created me to be a race car driver. I know it sounds funny, but I really do wonder if I am addicted to adrenaline. (Don't worry, I don't have a string of speeding tickets on my record. Just one that I can remember.) So I guess it was natural enough when I decided I wanted to study engineering after high school graduation.

It just so happened that I was accepted into the University of North Carolina at Charlotte in their new Motor Sports Engineering program. I was thrilled! And I loved every minute of it, except some of the math classes. Every afternoon, it seemed, I was rebuilding carburetors, designing engine components, or fabricating something for a race car. Every weekend was consumed with going to different race tracks and occasionally getting to drive a little—which only fueled my addiction. (If you have never driven a race car, let me just say you are missing out!)

I began to move up through the ranks pretty fast for a beginner. I started volunteering at Hendrick Motor Sports just to get my foot in the door and build relationships...and it worked! I began to meet a ton of famous people, and it seemed that everywhere I turned I was working with NASCAR research and development engineers and being trained by elite NASCAR drivers and mechanics. I was living my dream, and just when I thought it could not get any better, it did!

Blinded by the Light

The Spring semester of my freshman year, I applied for a job at Yates Racing which, at the time, was the owner of the 88 Dale Jarrett car. All my friends applied too, hoping for this chance of a lifetime. I went through the interviews and to my amazement was offered the position. They told me I would receive $10 an hour while in school, and as soon as I finished school, I would be paid $80,000 a year. Could life get any better?

I prayed about this and talked to my parents, but after realizing I didn't have a place to stay for the summer, I declined the job and told them I wanted to get more machining experience—which meant that I would program huge machines called lathes to cut metal. I thought it would be better for my career if I actually knew how to run the machines and not just diagram the engine components.

I moved back to my hometown and was quickly hired; in fact, I started work the next week. At this particular company, I was able to be around people who cut metal for everything from dental tools to landing gear for fighter jets. I mainly made parts for cigarette filter machines. And while I know that doesn't sound very appealing, I loved every minute because I had a goal to be the best engineer possible.

Reflection

As I look back upon the career path I had chosen, I realize that I had pursued it for all the wrong reasons: mainly money and pride. For some reason I felt that I had to prove myself by succeeding in every aspect of my life. Most of my family did not have an education, so I wanted to be the first to earn a Master's Degree in Engineering. In addition, a majority of my family didn't make a lot of money, so I wanted to prove that I could be wealthy if I so chose.

Another deciding factor was that I didn't want to be in ministry like my father. I loved God and wanted to serve within the church, but I had no interest in being a pastor. I had seen the abuse my family had taken, and to be honest, I was a bit jaded toward it all. I remember telling my father right before I left for school that besides him, there was not one man in our church that I wanted to follow spiritually because everyone seemed so fake.

In its place, my life had become consumed with fulfilling my dreams and plans, despite everybody telling me that I was a leader and that they could envision me leading people closer to Christ. My eyes were blinded to see, my ears deaf to hear what God wanted for my life. I did what I wanted to do and said what I wanted to say (Remember that phrase. We will refer back to it later on).

The Path

As I stated above, I had "chosen a career path." That idea seems rather normal in our society. We frequently ask children what they want to be when they grow up. Teenagers enrolling in college are required to pick a career path for which they will study. Now, I don't believe that this practice is wrong necessarily. The problem begins when we choose a path based upon our own agenda rather than on God's.

In my case, I had chosen my path based upon my own selfish vision. So let me pose you this question, "What path are you walking?" Before you answer in terms of an occupation or by dreaming about your ideal job, I want you to dig deeper. What is the motive behind your path? Is each step that you are treading leading you toward God and his best for your life? Or away from it?

Throughout this book we will begin a journey together. Picking up this book and reading the first chapter is your first step. Every path has an end, but the final destination cannot be the primary focus at this point. Imagine walking up a path to reach the summit of a mountain. While each of us envisions the panoramic view from the top and the brisk breezes blowing upon our faces with its accompanying sense of accomplishment, think of all the views along the way! If your imagination is limited to the summit, you will miss the beauty of the journey each step of the trek there.

It's true! Each step invites a lesson. Each trial and strenuous moment enables us to see God's strength and provision in spite of our weakness (see 2 Corinthians 9:8). Jesus commented that this path is difficult and not frequently traveled when he said, "For the gate is narrow and the way is hard that leads to life, and those who find it are few" (Matthew 7:14). My invitation to you is to join me on the path to create an *altared* culture. A culture of true worship.

Defining a Worship Culture

Before we embark on this journey, let me clearly explain what comprises a culture. Culture is defined by time, location, community, uniqueness, and a method of communication. So, a picture of one culture can look vastly different from another due to the enormity of its parameters. Each person is surrounded by a huge assortment and variety of cultures. We often refer to our society as a whole as American culture, but the truth is that it is made up of many concentric circles that impact our individual daily experiences.[i] Andy Crouch states, "Culture is, first of all, the name of our relentless, restless human effort to take the world as it's given to us and make something else."[ii]

We are called to create a culture around us based upon the worship of God (see Matthew 28:19-20). The purpose of this culture is help people engage in worship beyond the corporate worship service. To teach them how to hear and see what God is doing and carry it out in every relationship and situation they encounter. To present something new and more compelling to the world than what they have seen before.

The culture of worship I am describing will be identified as an *altared* culture. The Old Testament altar was a place of worship as well as remembrance. Just as the altar represented worship of God, this newly proposed culture will lead people to worship and remember in the same way. The remembrance will lead to greater faith due to the acknowledgment of God's faithfulness in the past, which will enable those who participate to worship in every aspect of their lives.

Skeptical? Not a problem. Sound impossible? I believe not. But come along and see for yourself.

Section 1: The Culture Jesus Lived

The reason I believe it is possible for us to create such a thing is that Jesus modeled the *altared* culture for us during his life. The values are those Jesus exemplified in his own journey of worship: dependency, desperation, and obedience. He effectively modeled worship of his Father in such way that it created a culture around him, a culture of people following his example of dependency, desperation, and obedience. We will unpack this more in chapters two through four.

Notice that Jesus teaches and develops his culture within the temple (see Matthew 26:55) and among the crowds (see Matthew 4:23-25), as well as withdrawing to worship God individually (see Mark 1:35). In essence, he lived a life of worship in every aspect, circumstance, and relationship. It is important to note this fact because Jesus would not have modeled a life of worship if it were not possible for us to obtain it through the power of his Holy Spirit (see John 14:12). God created us in his image and desires that we model the example that he set before us in his Son. The question is not, *Has God empowered us to create such a culture?* The question is, *Are you willing to accept his call to create culture with him?*

Section 2: First Steps

In my own life, I became willing to walk this path toward creating culture, but it came only after many substantially painful blows to my original plan. Some of you reading this book have chosen a path, as I did, that is leading you farther from God rather than towards worship. That theme has been common to all humanity throughout history. The prophet Jeremiah spoke, "Thus says the Lord: 'Stand by the roads, and look, and ask for the ancient paths, where the good way is; and walk in it, and find rest for your souls.' But they said, 'We will not walk in it'" (Jeremiah 6:16).

The initial steps toward creating a culture are often marked with resistance due to our own pride and arrogance. Jesus said, "For the gate is wide and the way is easy that leads to destruction, and those who enter by it are many" (Matthew 7:13). There are many different individual paths that a person can walk, but they all converge into one way: the way that is rooted in love for self rather than love for God. This path is a dead end. Each individual has to make a choice before the journey can commence: *Am I willing to surrender my charted course to walk another path?* If you are, then let the expedition begin!

Section 3: The Path to a New Culture

As we begin to walk this path, there are lessons to be learned and experiences to be had. Throughout this section of the book I will introduce different mileposts that I have encountered during my journey. The purpose of a milepost is to mark a moment in time: to remember the last mile traveled and to look forward to the unknown mile that awaits. It is important that we take these moments to stop, pause, and rest. If the moments are forgotten or not given value, then they will be lost. As I stated earlier, each step of the journey is important; without each individual step it is impossible to reach our destination.

The mileposts ahead include learning about surrender, identity, childlike faith, rest, and remembrance. I will refer to these mileposts as *altaring* moments. Punctuating the story of his people, God called them to remember him and give thanks along their journey. Altars dotted the landscape as memorial markers of remembrance for what had taken place. When the Israelites came upon desperate situations, the altars would serve as a memorial beacon, reminding them that the future would be secure because God had proven himself in the past.

Just like the Israelites, we need to identify *altaring* moments to serve as memorial mileposts along our journey. We need to pause and remember what God has done previously; this builds the faith we need to create the culture God desires. This ultimately leads to an *altared* culture: A culture that acknowledges God's goodness and greatness and has worship at its epicenter.

Section 4: Our Culture Destination

This newly proposed culture is centered upon worship. It is based upon the idea that Christ-followers everywhere are learning the relationship between individual and corporate worship and replicate that culture in every aspect of their lives. In essence, we are all called to lead others in the worship of God wherever we are. Rest assured, this task is one for which we are well equipped.

In this section of the book we will explore the fact that we are created in the image of God, and we therefore have the ability to create because he created. Not only has he created us for worship, he desires that we lead others to do the same. When we are experiencing this culture of authentic worship, we are empowered to lead and invite others into this same culture. And this cultural transfer will paint a picture to the world that they have never seen before.

Take the Next Step

It is important to understand that this journey is not achieved in a moment, just as a summit is not reached instantaneously. There are several progressive steps that must be taken and internalized for this book to accomplish its purpose. This book is one that needs to go deep, and each chapter should lead you to personally reflect on the material you just read.

Before you move on to the next step, I encourage you to make sure you not only comprehend the ideas mentally, but that you also embrace them in your soul. Remember, a culture is not determined by an individual experience. Culture is comprised of and functions within the context of a community. For that reason the topics of this book will need to be discussed with those around you who desire to create that same culture of worship.

The mistake that people have made countless times throughout history is to live life based upon their own agenda...rather than what flows out of the heart of God. I can identify because, as I stated earlier, my dream was all about my own mission. My path led me toward self-worship rather than pointing me upon the worship of God. I encourage you to not make the same mistake. Don't worry if you have been on that path; there is grace for you, just as there was for me. I invite you to take the next step and start a new path, a new journey with awesome purpose for your life!

Application

As you have read this chapter, I am sure you have identified different paths you have traveled that left you desiring more. As you think about those paths, ask God to show you how he was working in your life then, even when you were following your own agenda.

It could also be that you are knowingly walking a path in the wrong direction. I encourage you to pause and really evaluate if it will be worth it in the end. If you decide to walk towards God, know that he will be there, running to greet you and give you his best. If you find yourself in that place, read Luke 15:11-32 and embrace the Father's unconditional love for you.

If you are already walking the path towards God, ask him to speak to you as you read and show you specifically what to do with this material.

Finally, wherever you currently reside on this path, there is an opportunity for you to take a step in the right direction. Choose the path that leads to life. Discover the uncharted landscape of the *altared* culture of worship. Let the journey begin!

Chapter 2

Where You Go, I Go

"God!" I cried, "I will do anything you want. You can have my whole life...if you just let me keep my fingers."

The day had started like most every other day of my life. I had just celebrated my birthday the previous day, and I headed off to work that hot, sticky July morning excited at the prospect of all this nineteenth year of my life would entail. As it turned out, this particular day would entail a lot.

As soon as I arrived, my supervisor asked me to change the air chuck out of a lathe and set it up for a new operation. Wow, it was my first big opportunity! I had always been able to run the machine but had never set it up! I'd been trained by my supervisor many times, and I had watched experienced machinists do this routinely. I got all my tools, prepared myself for the task ahead of me, and climbed into the big intimidating machine.

Yes, I said, "climbed into." These particular machines are about as big as a car, so you can imagine that its parts are pretty big and heavy. The air chuck's function is to hold the part while the machine performs jobs or cuts on the piece of metal. This particular chuck weighed around 80 pounds.

As I entered the lathe, I loosened all the bolts that held the chuck in place, just I had been trained, and then proceeded to disengage the chuck. As I pushed the foot pedal to disengage it, both of my hands were wrapped around the chuck in order to pull it off. But something went wrong, and the chuck did not disengage.

I didn't know what to do and started to panic. I could only think of two options: I could either take my hand off the chuck and let it drop on my foot, and crush it, or I could hold on to the chuck and let it crush all my fingers. I chose number two, but—let's be honest—neither scenario was going to end well!

The machine began to pull my hands in between two pieces of metal which clamped at about 1,500 pounds of force. I know you are probably cringing, just thinking about it. To be honest, my body is actually shaking while I recall these horrific memories. Let's press on; we can do this because the story eventually does end well. Just as you can imagine, six of my fingers were crushed in the machine. As time faded into slow motion, I remember swearing as my fingers exploded under the pressure.

Desperation

I am sure you have heard that when people have bad accidents, their body creates a wash of adrenaline, which covers a lot of pain. Well, it's true. As my body reeled in the shock from my fingers being crushed, I was able to disengage the machine with my foot and go tell my supervisor that I needed to go to the hospital. After he recovered from almost passing out himself, he helped me get in his car and rushed me to the hospital. The pain had not yet hit, although I was coming in and out of consciousness. I just kept asking over and over, "Do you think they will have to amputate my hands?" He answered frantically, "I don't know; they look pretty bad."

Darts of fear began to pierce my soul, their poison racing throughout my being as my mind frantically churned through all the functions that required my fingers. Would I be able to eat?

Would I be able to feel or pick up anything? What job could I do? I definitely would never be able to play my guitar or piano again. I don't know if I can describe the cataclysmic sense of loss I experienced in those moments...or if words can even do it justice. I was scared out of my mind.

Eventually, I began to shake under the pain as I cried out in more desperation than I had ever known, "God, please, please. Please don't let me lose my fingers. I know I have done things wrong, but honestly, I love you. If you let me keep my fingers, I will serve you every day of my life. You can have all of me! I will be totally and wholly yours to do with whatever you like."

I wish I could say that angels filled the car and that my hands were miraculously healed in an instant of euphoric peace, but I can't. In its place, however, I did know that I had faith and that I could trust God with my life. But I had no idea what the next few moments would bring as they raced toward me like a speeding car. I looked at my supervisor and said quietly, "I know you don't understand this, and you are going to think I am crazy, but this is going to be one of the biggest blessings of my life. God is good, and He is working all things together for my good." He stared at me in disbelief, not understanding the act of worship that was taking place in my life at that moment.

The Essence of Worship

The goodness of God has been a constant in my life. And worshiping is one of the ways my heart has always connected most powerfully with God…and his goodness. Now, years later, I find myself serving and experiencing enormous joy as a Worship Pastor. I get paid—crazy as it sounds—to do what I love most: lead people into the presence of God. But a life of worship requires something. Actually, it requires everything! And it wasn't until I hit that point of desperation in the emergency room that I was willing to give everything to God as an act of worship.

When I think about what worship is and how it is defined in my life, I always refer back to some words that Jesus spoke about his own authority. John 5:19-20 says, "Truly, truly, I say to you, the Son can do nothing of his own accord, but only what he sees the Father doing. For whatever the Father does, that the Son does likewise. For the Father loves the Son and shows him all that he himself is doing." Can you see it? Jesus has given himself without reservation into the will of God.

And that is worship! In essence Jesus is saying, "I can do nothing in my own strength. So, whatever you're doing, I am going to do it. Whatever you say, I am going to say it. God, wherever you go, I want to go too!"

The context of this verse is Jesus healing a man on the Sabbath, which the Jewish religious leaders saw as breaking God's law. Jesus, on the other hand, used these healings as proof of his deity, proof of his connection with God. He was proclaiming that his actions were not initiated by his own independent authority; he was completely dependent on what God himself was doing.

Dependency on the Father was the essence of a life of worship for Jesus—and it is no less true for me or for you. Jesus points out this truth throughout the book of John and clearly states it again after he tells his disciples, "The words that I say to you I do not speak on my own authority, but the Father who dwells in me does his works" (John 14:10).

#1 Worshipper

Now correct me if I am wrong, but I'm guessing that if I were to take a poll on who was the greatest worshipper of God of all time, Jesus would win, hands down. I refer to him as the "number one worshipper" because he faultlessly exemplified a dependent life. Now he does have a slight edge on us because he is God (see John 1:1 and Colossians 1:15-20), which means he is perfect in every way, but nevertheless, he was also just as human as we are. When he came to earth, he laid aside his divine prerogatives, humbled himself, and walked among us (see Philippians 2:8).

So if Jesus' life shows us what the life of a worshipper looks like, shouldn't that same humility and dependency mark our worship? Shouldn't the cry of our heart be, "God, whatever you are doing, I want to do; whatever you are saying, I want to say?" You may have never entertained that thought before. Does that reflect your heart's desire? Some of us hunger powerfully for this in our inmost being yet feel frustrated; we see little evidence of God speaking and acting in our world or lives.

That explains perfectly the place I was in before my accident. I knew God existed, I knew all the stories, and I had engaged in the moral ideologies of Christianity, but I was not convinced that God was actively speaking and acting in my life. It wasn't until I got to the place of utter desperation that I began to start this journey toward a heart of dependent worship. Until that point in time I had primarily depended upon myself and my own abilities to make life work, but the sobering fact of the accident made me come to the realization that life was only found through dependency on God.

In that moment of fearful uncertainty, I gave up my own path to find life and embraced his. I wanted everything that God wanted for me as I submitted to him and cried out, "If you let me keep my fingers, I will serve you every day of my life." Now, you will probably notice that, even in my desperation, I still had a condition: keeping my fingers. But nevertheless, God brought me to a place of decision, and I was moving in the right direction. My desperation opened me to the will of God in a whole new dimension.

Even Jesus modeled a desperation that led him to solely depend on his Father. You might be wondering, "Was Jesus not fully complete in deity?" Of course, Jesus was fully God; what I am saying is that Jesus satisfied, delighted, and fed himself with what the Father was doing and saying. Jesus claimed, "Man shall not live on bread alone, but every word that comes from the mouth of God" (Matthew 4:4). I am arguing that dependency and joyful submission is what worship is truly about. Listen to the dependency in Jesus' cry when he said,

"My Father, if it be possible, let this cup pass from me; nevertheless, not as I will, but as you will" (Matthew 26:39).

Transformation

It is an easy cop-out to say, "Well, he was Jesus; he could do that because he was perfect," and dismiss ourselves from the very thing that Jesus was modeling for us. Do you think Jesus would have set an example for us to worship like this if it were not possible? Absolutely not! Jesus demonstrated through his actions and words that dependency upon God's voice and action is what worship looks like. In other words, "Follow me!"

If that sounds hard, well, I have good news. God is making it easier for us. Listen to this transformative language, "And we all, with unveiled face, beholding the glory of the Lord, are being transformed into the same image from one degree of glory to another. For this comes from the Lord who is the Spirit" (2 Corinthians 3:18). Jesus understood his identity and his dependency upon God. Just as Jesus didn't do or say anything unless he saw his Father doing it, he is transforming us into that same image.

Paul reminds us, "For in Christ all the fullness of Deity lives in bodily form, and you have *been given fullness* in Christ, who is the head over every power and authority" (Colossians 2:9-10 NIV, emphasis added). We are becoming a reflection of Christ, and the best part of the story is that we are not doing it. We can't do it! It is his Spirit that is bringing about the change within us, making us genuine worshippers.

Everything is Going to be Alright

As I sat in the emergency room, reeling and shaking in pain, the doctor looked at my hands and said, "You are about 1mm away from losing six of them from the first knuckle up, but I think I can save them. You're going to be okay." Relieved,

I sat back and thanked God over and over for letting me keep my fingers.

You know, as I often sit back and think about my relationship with Christ, I have to say that that was one of the greatest days of my life. Those lessons, as God brought me to the edge of desperation, have impacted every part of who I am. He started me on a path, the journey to become a true worshipper and create an *altared* culture, centered upon the worship of God. This is a culture of people who find sole satisfaction in Christ alone. I would not say that I have arrived, but I am in pursuit of the One who sustains my life.

And God is also bringing you to that point—to the place where you will say, "I can do nothing on my own, but only what I see my Father doing in the world today. For whatever He does, I follow and do. Whatever he says, I say." Take heart and believe it is possible because Jesus promises us, "The sheep [us] hear his voice, and he calls his own sheep by name and leads them out...and the sheep follow him, for they know his voice (John 10:3,4).

The first value that we must embrace in a culture of worship is dependency upon the correct source. My purpose is to inspire and equip you to live in an *altared* culture of worship—a culture that affects everything you do and everyone around you. God is transforming you into the image of his Son. He is inviting you into the intimacy of this culture so that he can show himself through you to the world, but it can only be accomplished through following his lead!

Application

I encourage you today as you read this book to pause, put the book aside, and re-live moments from times of desperation in your own life. How did you respond to crisis? Did you run to Christ? If so, what did you learn? If you ran to yourself, a substance, an idea, or a person, how did it leave you feeling at the end of it all?

Now invite God into those places in your life. Be vulnerable and trust his goodness toward you.

Finally, ask God to bring about this desire and desperation within your soul. Acknowledge that you can't step into a culture of worship in your own strength; ask for the transforming power that only he can provide.

Wait patiently, and over time you will begin to change. You probably won't even know it. Those around you will inform you that you have been transformed before their eyes. Be encouraged; God wants to do this through you. Invite him and give him permission to rule your actions as you walk through your life this week.

Chapter 3

Water, Water, Everywhere... But Not a Drop to Drink

The sun beat down upon me as I strained for every step. It was one of the most bizarre experiences I had ever encountered. One minute I was walking through a shadow as cold gusts of air chilled me to the bone, the next I was covered with sweat as I almost literally felt my skin turning red. Every step was a monumental feat. Every drop of moisture seemed to have boiled out my pores.

I glanced down and rummaged through my pack. Yeah, just as I expected—I was running low on water. If I didn't ration it carefully during this last leg of the journey, things could get dangerous fast. So I restrained my desire to guzzle the entire bottle in an instant. *Where was this guy,* you might be wondering? I was asking myself the same question as I hiked through the Annapurna range of the Himalayan Mountains: "What in the world am I doing here?"

I had trained for months, running nearly every day, hoping to get my body ready for the mountains in Western Nepal, only to find my preparations inadequate to the challenge at hand. Each step of the trek left my mouth drier, and there was no clean water to be found. Most of the local water would leave me bent over the side of the trail or worse...laid up in a bed. It was pure, clean water that I craved and needed so desperately. One of the lessons I learned that day was that my spirit needs to worship as much as my body needs to drink.

Water, Water, Everywhere... But Not a Drop to Drink

Parched

As we continue to excavate this idea of creating an *altared* culture of worship, let's go back to the One who modeled worship perfectly. As we said in the last chapter, Jesus himself was dependent to do and say exactly what his Father prompted (see John 5:19-20). To illustrate this further, Scripture uses a metaphor centered on the basic human need for food and water. I am not entirely sure why, but I think one major component is that hunger and thirst are common to every man, woman, and child. It does not matter who you are: rich or poor, American or non, young or old, tall or short, beautiful or plain...every person experiences these basic human needs!

Jesus was hitting on something central to our experience here, and it deserves our attention. Listen to him speak to a thirsty woman of questionable moral character.

> "So he came to a town of Samaria called Sychar, near the field that Jacob had given to his son Joseph. Jacob's well was there; so Jesus, wearied as he was from his journey, was sitting beside the well. It was about the sixth hour. There came a woman of Samaria to draw water.
>
> "Jesus said to her, "Give me a drink." (For his disciples had gone away into the city to buy food.) The Samaritan woman said to him, "How is it that you, a Jew, ask for a drink from me, a woman of Samaria?" (For Jews have no dealing with Samaritans.) Jesus answered her, "If you knew the gift of God, and who it is that is saying to you, 'Give me a drink,' you would have asked him, and he would have given you living water."

31

"The woman said to him, "Sir, you have nothing to draw water with, and the well is deep. Where do you get that living water? Are you greater than our father Jacob? He gave us the well and drank from it himself, as did his sons and his livestock." Jesus said to her, "Everyone who drinks of this water will be thirsty again, but whoever drinks of the water that I will give him will never be thirsty forever. The water that I will give him will become in him a spring of water welling up to eternal life." The woman said to him, "Sir, give me this water, so that I will not be thirsty or have to come here to draw water" (John 4:4-15).

Now fast-forward to the end of the story. Jesus said to her…

"You worship what you do not know; we worship what we know, for salvation is from the Jews. But the hour is coming, and is now here, when the true worshippers will worship the Father in spirit and truth, for the Father is seeking such people to worship him. God is spirit, and those who worship him must worship in spirit and truth" (John 4:21-24).

I know that most of us have read this story many times and have heard it used as a focal point of many messages, but I would like to look at it in a fresh way. Notice that Jesus is describing himself in this passage when he says that God is seeking out worshipers who worship in spirit and truth. Jesus was this kind of worshipper. And if Jesus is our example, which he is, then Jesus is modeling how we are to approach God; as the number one worshipper, Jesus is saying, *"Worship God like this!"*

Water, Water, Everywhere... But Not a Drop to Drink

Often we are so busy trying to figure out what in the world "spirit and truth" mean that we forget Jesus is demonstrating the authentic worship of the Father we are meant to emulate. Also, notice the strong correlation between water, thirst, and worship in what Jesus said. This isn't just an object lesson or an empty metaphor; Jesus is touching the core of this woman's being. By starting with her physical need, he uncovers her spiritual need to find satisfaction and source in God alone.

This illustration points us to the next element of a worship culture: desperation. Have you ever met a hungry or thirsty person? If not, it will become obvious very quickly that they are desperate to gratify their desire for food or water. In the same way Jesus was instructing us to quench our spiritual cravings at the only Source that can satisfy.

The Source

The more my days turn into years, the more I am convinced that God must be our uncontested source in order for true worship to occur. I not only see this played out in my daily life, I also see it throughout the story of God's people. During the time of the Old Testament there was a controversial figure among the Israelites. While kings and prophets were proclaiming that everything in the nation was fine, a man named Jeremiah began to speak for God.

Jeremiah's message was the exact opposite of the popular mindset of his culture. While others spoke of peace, this troublemaker warned of the destruction of Jerusalem and the very nation because of their wayward hearts and stiff-necked pride. Jeremiah used a water metaphor as well, claiming the people had dug underground storage tanks that could not actually hold water. Their best efforts were, in fact, useless.

"My people have committed two sins: They have forsaken me, the spring of living water, and have dug their own cisterns, broken cisterns that cannot hold water" (Jeremiah

2:13). Again, we see water used to illustrate our relationship with God. As a matter of fact, this idea permeates to the very last words of Scripture. One of the final invitations in the book of Revelation is this: "The Spirit and the Bride say, 'Come.' And let the one who hears say, 'Come.' And let the one who is thirsty come; let the one who desires take the water of life without price" (Revelation 22:17).

Okay, we can see that spiritual thirst is clearly a prevailing theme in the Bible, but what does water have to do with an *altared* culture? Look again at Jesus' example. Why would he tell us about free living water if he hadn't already drunk from the source himself? Jesus, as human as you and I, had all the same bodily needs we experience every day. His invitation is to not only thirst but to be filled!

Jesus challenges us to worship by desperately desiring to be satisfied from the source of true life. If we venture back to Jesus' earlier comment that "God is spirit, and those who worship him must worship in spirit and truth," we might just find that Jesus was talking about a way of life! A culture of worship that is centered on thirst and anchored in the desperation, the determination to be fully satisfied from the one and only source, God himself. Every act, every decision we make to source our lives in Christ is a step toward building and sustaining an *altared* culture of worship.

If we look at the beginning of Jesus' public ministry, we see that God led him into the wilderness to solidify this desperation in his own soul.

> "Then Jesus was led up by the Spirit into the wilderness to be tempted by the devil. And after fasting forty days and forty nights, he was hungry. And the tempter came and said to him, "If you are the Son of God, command these stones to become loaves of bread." But he answered, "It is written, Man shall not live by

bread alone, but by every word that comes from the mouth of God" (Matthew 4:1-4).

Before Jesus could create an *altared* culture, he had to understand desperation in the core of his being. Without the desperation to feed and satisfy himself solely with the words proceeding out of the mouth of God, it would be impossible to withstand the pressures and temptations of the enemy. The task of creating a culture of people that would worship his Father was too great without accepting this profound truth. He had to satisfy his own hunger with the correct source.

So Hungry I Can Almost Taste It

As I run through different memories in my mind, I can't remember a time when I was really, truly hungry. To be honest, I think that most Americans have difficulty relating to Jesus' comments and teaching on hunger. Our wealth has actually allowed us to be overfed so that we often complain to others, "I think I ate too much!" Nevertheless, we need to explore this idea of hunger because, again, Jesus would not have talked about it if it weren't central to the Father's heart for us.

Dig through these simple words that Jesus instructed us to pray, "Give us this day our daily bread" (Matthew 6:11). What do they mean? Do we really need to pray for our daily bread? Don't we have more than enough at every meal, and to be honest, who wants to eat just a loaf of bread? I think there is far deeper meaning just below the surface, and I want to invite you deeper to discover the root of worship.

One afternoon my mentor challenged me with two key thoughts on this passage. First, why does Jesus' prayer have "day" and "daily" in the same sentence? Why? Because this statement refers to both quantity and frequency. "Daily bread" refers to how much bread we are supposed to ask for: enough to sustain our daily hunger. The second component of the statement, "give us this day," refers to how often we are supposed to venture out to find the bread.

I believe that Jesus was referring to actual bread, but remember that he also spoke of another source that satisfied his other hunger—"I have food to eat that you know nothing about" (John 4:32). Again, Jesus is showing us how to become a worshipper. When we desperately seek to satisfy our hunger for him daily, we are closest to our Father...which results in intimacy...which is God's desire from the beginning (see Genesis 3:8).

There is another component of this simple phrase worth sifting through. Jesus referenced God's provision of manna (bread) for the Israelites while they were in the desert. He reminded the people of this correlation when he said, "Your forefathers ate the manna in the desert" (John 6:41). Not only do these words refer to God becoming our source, but they also call us to remembrance. He is reminding us that God always provides for our spiritual and physical needs. We can be very forgetful.

Jesus then said to them, "Truly, truly, I say to you, it was not Moses who gave you the bread from heaven, but my Father gives you the true bread from heaven" (John 6:31-32). This was an important teaching point for Christ because all of his listeners would have been familiar with manna, and now he wanted the crowd to connect that supernatural provision with himself. He was their source for nourishment! He was their manna. He emphasized this by declaring, "Here is the bread that comes down from heaven, which a man may eat and not die. I am the living bread that came down from heaven" (John 6:50-51).

Before we go any further with this thought, let's outline some facts about manna from Exodus 16.

1) "Manna" is Hebrew for "what is it?" (It was bread that the Lord gave them to eat.)
2) The Israelites had to rise early, venture out, and

harvest about two liters of it each and every morning.
3) They could gather as much as they could eat.
4) If they didn't gather it in the morning, the manna melted as the sun grew hot.
5) If they tried to store the manna, it would rot and get infested with worms.
6) God used manna to sustain the Israelites for forty years.
7) This symbol was important enough for God to instruct Moses to place a jar of it inside the Ark of the Covenant as a memorial to God's provision.

I think it's safe to say that manna is a big deal to God. "Why is that?" you might ask. Well, I am not telling you to get up extra early tomorrow and head out to the front lawn. What God has to offer us now is far better: Jesus is our bread! Jesus told the crowd, "'For the bread of God is he who came down from heaven and gives life to the world.' They said to him, 'Sir, give us this bread always.' Jesus said to them, 'I am the bread of life, whoever comes to me shall not hunger and whoever believes in me shall never thirst'" (John 6:35-37). Worship is nothing more or less than hungering for God. And God is absolutely determined to satisfy the thirsty soul of the worshipper.

The Presence

A few months ago I had a recurring dream over the course of a single night. Dreaming is not uncommon for me. Ever since I was child, I can have as many as five or six distinct dreams in one evening. They are never bad dreams; they are usually just about everyday life.

On this particular night I kept replaying one specific dream, and I felt God was using this dream to speak to me. Now, my personal theological background would never support the crazy notion of God speaking in a dream...because

God has said everything he needs to say in the Scriptures, and Scripture is closed. While I still believe that God's Book is complete, I have learned to open my heart and be sensitive to what God continues to speak. Going back to an earlier thought, if Jesus didn't do anything outside of what he saw his father doing, and if I am supposed to follow his worshipping example, then I have to believe that God's Spirit will instruct and counsel me in the same way he did Jesus (John 14:26).

Back to the dream, I remember hearing this phrase: "Where my manna is, there my presence is found." The first time I recalled it, I just shook it off in a dazed semi-slumber. The second time I actually woke up and said to myself, *That might be God, Eric. You need to remember that statement.* So I prayed through those words for a few days and looked through Scripture to find any references to manna. And I settled upon this thought: When I come to feast upon Christ (the bread/manna) daily, I am fulfilled and satisfied, and I experience his presence. Jesus is offering himself to me as the source that satisfies all hunger and thirst...and in that place his presence is found.

I challenge you to look through Scripture at what happens to people when they come into the presence of Christ in his glorified state. It's the same every time. They fall upon their face as if they were dead. (Remember the apostle John in the book of Revelation?) And that is what worship is—bowing our knee, prostrating ourselves before our Creator, and embracing his rule of our lives.

Let's look back at Jesus' words, "Give us this day our daily bread," in light of what we now know about the correlation between himself and manna. Jesus, as the unceasing bread of life, is inviting us to come each and every day to be satisfied in him alone. We can eat as much as we like until we have had our fill. There are things he is saying and doing today, and he wants to show them to us through his Spirit that lives within us as believers; if we don't pursue him, we will miss this priceless opportunity.

Water, Water, Everywhere... But Not a Drop to Drink

We can't just understand some things *about* Jesus and live in the false belief that we know him. We can't just be content with the bread we ate last year, last week, or even yesterday. It isn't enough.

We have to satisfy our hunger each and every day! God sustained the people of Israel for forty years as they wandered in a dry, dusty, and weary land. As they roamed, parched and hungry, he was faithful to feed them...but only if they searched out the bread that was crucial to their survival.

In the same way, your survival and perseverance through this life is sourced by God and his ability to satisfy your hunger and quench your thirst. Life will be rough, and there are no guarantees, but a worshipper is able to find God in every circumstance. A perfect example is when Jesus was tempted by Satan in the desert. He was challenged to turn the rocks into bread...but Satan didn't know that Jesus had a greater source to satisfy his hunger (Matthew 4:3-4).

John Piper comments on this story, "The point of manna (bread) was this, Satan: Don't trust in bread nor even miracle bread—trust in God! Don't get your deepest satisfactions in this life from food—not even God-wrought miracle food—but from God. Every word that comes out of the mouth of God reveals God. And it is this self-revelation that we feed on most deeply. This will last forever. This is eternal life!"[iii]

Finally, just as God instructed Moses to put manna in the Ark of the Covenant for all the generations to remember, God has placed in you and me his Spirit who is our sustenance. The Spirit causes us to remember all the past provision of God and then to worship the One, the Source. And then lead others to do the same.

As we "eat" daily, Jesus promises that we will experience his presence. The first component of an *altared* culture (from the first chapter) is Jesus' mantra, "Where you go, I go." We identified that he lived with a moment-by-moment *dependency* that drew him closer to the Father. Now, the *desperation* that Jesus models here through hunger and thirst becomes the second component of this worship culture. Pursuit leads to presence...which begins to shape the foundation of this newly proposed culture. And as that culture is shared by a growing number of pursuers, then this worship culture begins to take root in the community.

Hunger and thirst are essential to the heart of a worshipper. Notice that every person experiences hunger and thirst; it is common to all mankind. You are not different from the rest of the world.

The difference lies in what you use to fill those desires. When you satiate that hunger with Christ himself, the results are good: "Blessed are those who hunger and thirst for righteousness, for they shall be satisfied" (Matthew 5:6). Not only will we be satisfied, we will actually live life to the fullest because "man shall not live by bread alone, but by every word that comes from the mouth of God" (Matthew 4:4).

Satisfied, But Longing For More

High in the Himalayans, I finally reached the small village of Jharkot where we found some purified water, and I gulped it down greedily. Without it, dehydration would have quickly ravaged me. I was exhausted from the trek, but my strength returned with each swallow of the delicious, replenishing water. That evening I was able to go work alongside a farmer in a field and share with him God's love as we talked about the parable of the sower.

As satisfying as the water had been that day, I had to come back again the next day to get more water to continue my journey. Fresh water for fresh thirst. As I pondered what was taking place in my body physically, I remembered what God had promised me about my spiritual journeys—that rivers of living water would come bubbling out of my "stomach" (see John 4:14). I simply prayed that God would continue to satisfy my deepest thirst. And he has.

Application

There is a slight possibility that you are expecting me to suggest a forty-day fast. After all, Jesus did it, right? Instead, I would simply ask you to evaluate your desires and discover where your hunger and thirsts are focused. Your focus could be affirmation, position, wealth, possessions...any number of self-directed goals. As God's Spirit begins to exhume those lifeless things from deep within you, surrender each one. Ask him to create desperation for himself that is stronger. As you do, you will begin to notice a pull of your heart toward God, and over time, those lesser things will begin to fade.

If you can't seem to shake your hunger for the counterfeits, pray against it. There is a good chance that you have made an agreement with the enemy and given that desire a foothold in your soul.

Simply take authority in Christ's name and live in the freedom that is already yours. This resurrection power was obtained for you by Christ when he conquered death and sin.

Finally, choose to fast from something you have leaned on in the past, something that used to sustain you for a period of time. In its place, let God strengthen your dependency on him. "Taste and see that the Lord is good; blessed is the man who takes refuge in him" (Psalm 34:8).

Chapter 4

It's the Beginning of Wisdom

A few months ago I watched the movie "Evan Almighty." Steve Carell, the character who plays Evan, is being called by God to build an ark, to be a modern-day Noah and save a neighborhood from the impending dam breakage that will flood most of the town. Now this obviously has no Scriptural basis, but I think the movie had many points that are applicable to our walk with God. One of those scenes still makes me laugh every time I think about it.

As Evan gets into his car, he looks in his rearview mirror, expecting to see the parking spot in which to back his car. Instead, he sees the character of God played by Morgan Freeman. Evan screams at the top of his lungs in fear, and God calmly states, "That's the beginning of wisdom." Although what was said was pretty humorous, it is based on a Scripture you might be familiar with: "The fear of the Lord is the beginning of wisdom" (Proverbs 1:7). Despite the humor, I think this is a pretty accurate understanding of what it means to fear the Lord.

As we have delved into Jesus' characteristics of worshipping, we have unearthed two main components so far. One, he had a dependency in his being upon whatever he heard or saw his Father doing. Second, he had desperation for the actual words that were proceeding out of the mouth of his Father. The third and final component that we will explore from his example is obedience.

If you really examine it, the root of the previous two characteristics is obedience as well. From the beginning, God instructed his people about obedience when he said, "You shall love the Lord your God with all your heart and with all your soul and with all your might. And these words that I command you today shall be on your heart" (Deuteronomy 6:5-6). If you love the One who created you with all your heart, soul, and mind, then you will certainly be both desperate and hungry. And you will be intent upon obeying the directions of your Creator. You will be an adoring and obedient worshipper.

When we look through Jesus' life, we see that he not only lived out this great commandment, he also instructed others to do the same (see Matthew 22:37). His life and ministry were the embodiment of loving obedience toward his Father. In Jesus' example we can see that fear equaled obedience. In other words, Jesus walked in holy fear of his Father, and it was a big deal to Jesus that we follow him in that same course toward whole-life abandonment to God.

Fear

But it's the concept of fear that gives us most trouble. We don't like the word, and it definitely has a bad connotation in our culture. We view fear as a childish mindset, one we desperately try to forget and refuse to talk about. Men boast that they have "no fear" and can conquer anything. Some people are even bold (or foolish) enough to put stickers on the car claiming to the world that they have "no fear."

Many individuals don't like to discuss their fears because of the vulnerability that ensues upon the telling of their secret. America is, after all, the home of the brave. We would never admit to cowering in fear of anything. There is no opponent or task too big for us to handle, right? That is obviously what our culture ingrains in us from an early age. This ideology even finds its way into the church and into our individual lives as well. It is this independent and rogue nature, however, that separates us from God. It robs us of the intimacy that is ours to be experienced with the One upon whom we rely for life itself.

As we can see throughout history, this is not a new concept, and God addresses the issue of human independence with every person. It's part of the culture of the world in which we live. On the other hand, Jesus calls us out of that broken culture to develop a brand new culture. When we look at his example, we see someone who had every reason to be independent, yet chose obedience to his Father's will (Philippians 2:5-8). He modeled a way of living that is rooted firmly in dependence and obedience. If Jesus was the number one worshiper, then it's logical for us to follow his example toward an *altared* culture of worship shaped by an obedient heart.

Fear – Defined

What in the world does the word "fear" mean in our context as worshipers? It's a great question that we must answer thoughtfully if we are to move forward in our pursuit. If you look up the word "fear" in a concordance you will discover that the word is used over 260 times throughout the Bible with a variety of different meanings based upon the context. As I began to research it, I became aware that I could write a book just with the information that I gathered on that topic!

The first word for fear that I want to mention is the Hebrew word *yir'ah*. It has three definitions that can change based upon the context: 1) fear or terror, 2) awesome or terrifying thing (the object causing fear), and 3) respect, reverence, or piety.[iv] In our context we will focus on the third definition. This is the meaning that is used throughout the book of Proverbs and specifically in the key verse where we started our discussion, "The fear of the Lord is the beginning of wisdom" (Proverbs 1:7).

This word is also found in the instruction of Psalm 2:11, "Serve the Lord with fear, and rejoice with trembling." I don't believe that Jesus is telling us that we are supposed to walk around shaking all of the time as we think of all the terror and horrors that God could rain down upon us...as some have erroneously believed. I believe he is inviting us to dig deeper, past our initial reservations into the awesome character of God himself. But first, let's look at the counterfeit.

Spirit of Fear

Throughout time there has been a force of darkness that seeks to thwart our view of God. That force, as you probably could guess, is Satan and his demons. One of the main components of his plan is to divert our allegiance, our fear, of God to that of other individuals. John Bevere puts it this way when he speaks on this diversion, "If you desire the praise of man, you will fear man. If you fear man, you will serve him – for you will serve what you fear."[v]

When you look at it this way, the truth can be rather sobering. The truth of the matter is that this darkness resides within us all, and we are battling it on many different planes: within our mind internally and within our culture externally. Paul reminded Timothy of this when he wrote, "For God gave us a spirit not of fear but of power and love and self-control" (2 Timothy 1:7). It is interesting to note that the Greek word for fear here, *deilia*, means timidity, fearfulness, or cowardice.[vi] Why would Paul have to remind Timothy of the distinction between the two definitions of fear?

Because the wrong view of fear is a lie and can cause us to disengage rather than engage with God and his plans for us. Satan's plan is for us to disengage and alienate ourselves from God so that we will buck up in pride and pretend that we don't need anything outside of ourselves. We can see the pride in this level of independence, but its foundation is based upon a lie that God can't be trusted, that we need to make life work in our own strength (aka, a spirit of fear, see Genesis 3:1-7). To illustrate this idea further I would like to share a story of my own.

The Hope of Glory

From a very early age I loved sports, baseball in particular. I was always the best guy on every team and received honors and accolades, such as being on the All-Star team every year. I don't think I was prideful because I really just loved the game and tried to give it my best effort every time I took the field.

As I moved into the high school glory years of my baseball career, I was excited and determined to excel at my sport. I lifted weights and ran every morning, got to school early to practice, and then practiced and ran again in the afternoons just to prepare. It finally came to the day for the final cut. The coach looked at me and said, "Eric, you are good enough, I just don't have a spot for you on the team." It hurt, but I could accept it because I was playing in two other leagues at that time.

I continued to prepare for the next year, playing almost year round. When the next chance came, I made the team and got to play a fair amount but still wasn't satisfied. Just as the previous year, I worked hard, waiting with anticipation for what my senior year would hold. A few days into the tryouts we had a former college pitcher come and throw at batting practice. I'm not going to lie, I was a bit nervous. It was my turn so I stepped up to the plate, gripped the bat tight and dug in with anticipation asking myself, "Am I even going to be able to hit this guy?"

First pitch I swung and hit a line drive homerun over the center field wall. I was ecstatic as all the players congratulated me with high fives and encouraging comments. The second time at bat, I hit a line drive off the left field fence. It was my dream, and I knew that all my hard work had paid off. That night I couldn't wait to get home to tell my parents, and I could barely sleep because of the excitement. I couldn't even imagine what the next day would hold. That day the coach called me to the dug-out, and I just knew it was to tell me I had earned a starting spot on the team. He looked me in the eye and said, "You are going to make the team, but you will never start."

Disengaged

Something devastating happened in my life that day. I bought a lie. Satan was sitting right beside me, enticing me to take the bait, and the lie I bought that day was, "If I stay disengaged, then I can't fail." It made sense to me. I had worked hard...and failed. I vowed to never go through that humiliation and hurt again. I decided to become passive and disengage because that was the only way I knew how to not experience the hurt. In that moment, I chose the wrong form of fear; I took on a spirit of fear and claimed it as my new identity.

This is exactly what Jesus is trying to protect us from and set us free from. A sprit of fear pervades the culture of the world. Fear often causes us to disengage from something or someone. Fear always alienates and separates us. Why do you think most people, including Christians, live so much of their life in guilt and shame? They have instinctively responded to fear with disengagement. As they have drifted away from Christ for lack of reverence, awe, and love for him, they have trusted in themselves instead. Which is Satan's very intent.

The lie rooted in fear goes something like this, "God could never love me after what I have done; it's all up to me, and I have failed." The spirit of fear builds a barrier that separates us from God, inch by inch, and inevitably disengages us from our own hearts. The disengagement sets us up for additional failure, and the anger over our failures leads us into greater fear. "'Those who are afraid draw back from Him, but those who fear Him draw toward Him."[vii] This leads us to the second part of our discussion: the intimacy that comes through a right fear of God.

Fear of the Lord

The fear of the Lord. Just those words alone leave many of us cowering with images of God waiting for us to make a mistake so he can punish us. It leaves others doubting at the core of their being that a God that must be feared could ever be trusted. But of course, the exact opposite is true, which we will see as we explore the inviting truth that Scripture intends. Jesus was not *afraid* of his Father; he *feared* him. Fear is rooted more in respect, reverence, and obedience than the negative connotations we attach to the word. A healthy view of fear results in a person being fully alive and intimately connected.

In the previous chapter, we discussed how Christ quenched his thirst in God. Jesus said that the water he gives would actually become a spring of water within us, welling up to eternal life (see John 4:14). We have already seen how Jesus used this metaphor of water to symbolize worship, but what if water could also represent fear? Well, it actually can, and the same relationship is seen in Proverbs 14:27, "The fear of the Lord is a fountain of life, turning a man from the snares of death." The reason why fear and worship are both characterized by water is that they are one and the same. Fear is worship and worship is fear.

Remember when we said that fear is about obedience and reverence, which results in intimacy, rather than our natural negative view of the word? David Peterson comments on this relationship when he states, "Acceptable worship means approaching or engaging with God on the terms that he proposes and in the manner that he makes possible. Although some of Scripture's terms for worship may refer to specific gestures of homage, rituals, or priestly ministrations, worship is more fundamentally faith expressing itself in obedience."[viii]

When you look at Jesus' life, you see one who expressed his worship to God by his obedience: "I don't do anything apart from my Father." Where did Jesus get this idea of obedience? Well, it isn't a new concept; it was outlined long ago when God first brought his people out of slavery in Egypt. As a matter of fact, it goes back even further to when Satan was cast out of heaven for his lack of obedience (Ezekiel 28: 2-10).

Samuel speaks about obedience in the Old Testament when he says, "Does the Lord delight in burnt offerings and sacrifices as much as in obeying the voice of the Lord? To obey is better than sacrifice." (1 Samuel 15:22). God has always been after our hearts from day one. The outward show of affection is meaningless if it does not have a foundation in love, reverence, and awe...which is shown through the action of obedience.

The truth of the matter is that most of us stink at obedience. We can keep enough rules to make people think we are holy, but most of us have never dealt with the deep uncovered places of our soul. Many of us have a problem with authority, which leads us toward rebellion. We tend to think we have something to prove, which is really rooted in the fact that we just don't trust that God is enough. Well, God has a solution to our problem that Jesus understood, "The fear of the Lord is the beginning of knowledge." When we truly begin to fear the Lord, he offers us something; he offers us himself. John Bevere comments,

> "The fear of the Lord is the beginning, or starting place, of an intimate relationship with God. Intimacy is a two-way relationship. For example, I know about the president of the United States. I can list information about his accomplishments and his political stance, but I do not actually know him. I lack a personal relationship with him. Although I'm a citizen of the United States and know about him, I could not speak to him as though he were my friend.

That would be inappropriate and even disrespectful."[ix]

We can use this example as we think about our relationship to God. If we do not fear the Lord, we only know *about* him. But he offers something far greater. Intimacy and friendship are ours for the taking if we approach God the same way Jesus demonstrated for us! Proverbs 25:14 says, "The secret of the Lord is with those who fear him." Remember, Jesus said he only did what he heard his father speaking. All throughout the New Testament we see this not only exemplified in Jesus' life, but also in the apostles and members of the early church. The Bible speaks of them hearing and experiencing God in miraculous ways. Could it be that God was revealing the intimate words that give life to them because of their fear?

Is it also possible that God is still speaking, that he wants to reveal the same secrets to you and me? I believe the answer to both of those questions is "Yes". When you begin to fear God, you engage intimately with the supernatural as he reveals his heart and desires to you. Jesus said we would be transformed by the renewing of our minds, that we can test and discern God's will (see Romans 12:2). The only way this is possible is through fear of the Lord. Godly fear brings intimate engagement.

Engaged

To worship God is to fear him, and to fear him is to obey him. God promises us that if we approach him as Jesus modeled, we will experience his friendship. "Friendship with the Lord is reserved for those who fear him. With them he shares the secrets of his covenant" (Psalm 25:14 NLT). The secret to Jesus' intimacy with the Father was his fear that exemplified itself in obedience. Jesus is inviting us to approach the Lord with fear, and through that intimate relationship he promises us that we will do even greater things than Jesus (see John 14:12). An *altared* culture is one of engagement. Jesus was fully engaged in every aspect of life. Most importantly, he intimately connected with his Source, which is only discovered through fear and obedience.

Application

I realize this might be a new and fresh way of looking at fear for you. It is quite possible that you have unearthed some lies and misconceptions about fear that you have believed for many years. Please know you are not alone. I invite you sit back, clear your mind, and ask God to show you where your view of him has been skewed by a deep-rooted lie. Ask God to show you where you are disengaging from him, others, or your own heart due to a spirit of fear.

Once you begin to identify some of those thoughts and places, simply ask God, "How should I view you and relate to you and others?" Pray through Jesus' examples and ask him to develop the fear of the Lord within you. Again, do not try to do this under your own strength; that is impossible. Only God's Spirit can bring about this change in you. Finally, be amazed as you learn to worship God through fear, which will lead you to the intimate secrets only the engaged experience.

Section 2
First Steps

Chapter 5

The Path to Intimacy

Over the years I have discovered something rather odd about myself. I like trails and paths. *Why is that?* you might ask. I am fascinated with a clearly marked pathway through uncertain and rough terrain. I love the adventure of what lies ahead.

When I was a child, I made trails through the clutter of toys scattered across my bedroom floor. A labyrinth of trails decorates the woods on my property; I even have trails through my flower bed. I painstakingly groom them to make sure they look just right, spreading mulch, cutting away obtruding branches, and clearing out the unwanted weed nuisance. Now, I could dismiss my fascination with trails as an obsessive compulsion or downright weirdness, but I believe that God has used it in my life to reveal an intricate detail concerning the *altared* culture of worship we're exploring.

The Path to a Culture of Worship

Over the past three chapters we have explored three components of worship that were displayed in Jesus' life: dependency, desperation, and obedience. We know that if we are going to create anything of substance, it must be founded upon the One who modeled the truest life of worship. As we venture into the next leg of our journey, we're going to talk about walking a path.

The Path to Intimacy

We often hear people speak of walking with God and if we are honest, many of us—including myself—are left wondering, "How do I do that?" As God revealed to me my own love for paths, I was drawn to this imagery throughout the Bible where it uses this metaphor for our relationship with God. In this next section of the book I will share with you how my path toward an *altared* culture began. I will also invite you to explore the possibilities God has for your journey. I invite you to take the next step with me on to the path of life!

The Path of Life

At several strategic moments within the story of human redemption, the idea of the path surfaces and resurfaces. These moments are not mere coincidence or chance. A path is a means by which we connect with God. There is a specific path upon which one must travel to experience intimacy with Christ. David declared of God, "You make known to me the path of life; in your presence there is fullness of joy; at your right hand are pleasures forevermore" (Psalm 16:11).

If God made the path of life known to David, he must also desire that we have this same understanding. So let's ask the question, *What is the path of life?* Our answer is also found in the book of Psalms. David prays, "Lead me in the path of your commandments, for I delight in it" (Psalm 119:35). Apparently, the path of life is actually the commandments of God. David then proclaims that on this path we will not walk a mediocre pace, but we will run in pursuit of God's commandments (see Psalm 119:35).

The Hebrew word for path that David uses is *derek*. This can mean road, way, or path. It also can be defined as a journey or direction. In essence, David is saying that he is journeying toward God by way of his commands. The more figurative meaning of *derek* is a course of life or moral character.[x] So, the path of life is not as much a physical path through an uncertain earthly terrain as it is a spiritual conduit through which we connect with God.

Unlike David, we do not operate under the Old Covenant. However, this does not mean that we are exempt from the commandments of God. The New Covenant through Jesus' death and resurrection allows us to meet all the requirements of God, but life is still found in his commands and instruction from the Old Testament.

In addition, I would argue that God continues to speak through his Word and his Spirit who lives within us. We know that Jesus is the same yesterday, today, and tomorrow (Hebrews 13:8). His instruction today is never contrary to what he has already said. His commands are still the way or path upon which we experience life. Jesus is the very essence of life: He came that we may have eternal life, and he obtained that life through conquering death (see John 3:16-17).

The Messenger

Before Jesus came on the scene, another prominent figure spoke about a path. John the Baptist fulfilled a prophecy of Isaiah to prepare the *way* of the Messiah (see Isaiah 40:3-5). Mark 1:2-3 states, "Behold I send my messenger before your face, who will prepare your *way*, the voice of one crying in the wilderness: 'Prepare the *way* of the Lord, make his paths straight.'"

John's purpose in the redemptive story was to put people's hearts in order, to clear the obstructions that would hinder the *new way* that was coming. He preached repentance and urged people to change their allegiance from themselves and their traditions to the coming Messiah. God knew that without this preparation, the hearts of his hearers would miss out, blinded by misunderstanding and disbelief. A path had to be made for the *new way* in the hearts of all who would listen, a way that would be controversial and opposite from what they had known.

The Narrow Way

Jesus included the idea of the path in his teachings as well. He referred to himself as "the way." He fulfilled the prophecy of Isaiah and the teaching of John the Baptist when proclaiming, "I am the way, and the truth, and the life, No one comes to the Father except through me" (John 14:6). Jesus also taught which path would lead to life: "Enter by the narrow gate. For the gate is wide and the *way* is easy that leads to destruction, and those who enter by it are many. For the gate is narrow and the *way* is hard that leads to life, and those who find it are few" (Matthew 7:13-14).

In this passage Jesus simply states that there are two paths. Although both carry us through the course of life, their final destinations are remarkably different. Also in great contrast is the level of resistance one encounters upon each path.

The word that Jesus uses in this scripture is the Greek word *hodos. Hodos* means a way, a traveled way, or a journey. Metaphorically speaking, it can mean a course of conduct or a manner of thinking and deciding.[xi] Look again at this Scripture through the lens of the word "*hodos*" that Christ used... "Enter by the narrow gate. For the gate is wide and the *way* is easy that leads to destruction, and those who enter by it are many. For the gate is narrow and the *way* is hard that leads to life, and those who find it are few."

First, Jesus is inviting us to enter the narrow gate. *What is the gate?* It is Jesus himself! John 10:5-9 says, "Truly, truly, I say to you, I am the door of the sheep. All who came before me are thieves and robbers, but the sheep did not listen to them. I am the door. If anyone enters by me, he will be saved..." Second, the resistance experienced on the way that leads to destruction is minimal. Along this path the decisions and manner of thinking are based on one's own perspective and desires. This way does not result in an individual finding life but rather in reaping the destructive consequences of a self-centered worldview.

Finally, Jesus he tells us that few people find the way of life because it is narrow and hard. Does that mean that Jesus intentionally made it hard and difficult to find life? *No!* I believe he is simply stating that he is the way of life and that few people are willing to walk this way to find intimacy with God. When we walk the path he desires, our conduct changes. He changes us to do and say what he is doing and saying. He also transforms our minds, which results in a new perspective that changes the way we make decisions (see Romans 12:2). No longer do we validate truth by our own opinions and choices; rather, we operate in the mind of Christ (see 1 Corinthians 2:16).

Why is this path hard? Because we are constantly tempted to wander from the markings of the path to pioneer other ways to find life. At times it may seem that we have stumbled upon a new path...when in reality, we have simply stepped onto the same road of ease and convenience that the world follows!

The Path of Destruction

The story that I shared at the beginning of the book is an example of the easy path in its truest form. Although I loved God and had attended church my entire life, I still desired to walk another path to find life. In our culture there is no shortage of paths that promise life; the problem is that most of them converge into this huge highway that leads us away from the relationship that we most desire. There are many paths that people are trekking down with great devotion, greatly desiring to experience life to the fullest.

In that sense, we already live in a culture of worship. Every person is created for this; they will perform the act of worship because it is in their nature. It is impossible not to worship! This reality is evident everywhere you turn: People worship sports teams weekly as they file into arenas in droves, eager to express their love and devotion. In our society people worship themselves, their careers, and their possessions. Just about any hobby or activity you can name—I am positive you can find someone out there who has devoted their whole life to it.

So you can see that worship is not the problem in itself. These examples reinforce how broad the path is that leads to destruction. The reason it is so difficult to walk the narrow path is that we are surrounded by the negative effects of another worshipping culture. The popular way is in direct opposition to the path Jesus marked toward true life. The *altared* culture I am introducing is one of many; the only difference is that this culture is founded upon the worship of God. This culture feeds us with the life of Christ and creates something the world has never seen. And the great news is that we have a helper to illuminate the sequential steps toward the destination we most desire.

The Helper

One can easily see that the way Jesus calls us to walk is in opposition to our flesh. Because of this, God has sent a helper to us in the person of his Holy Spirit. Jesus instructed us that we would receive a counselor and teacher to help us navigate the narrow path. In John 14:15-17 Jesus claims, "If you love me, you will keep my commandments. [Again we see a direct correlation between *the way* and keeping God's commandments]. And I will ask the Father, and he will give you another Helper, to be with you forever, even the Spirit of truth, whom the world cannot receive, because it neither sees him nor knows him [the *easy way*]. You know him, for he dwells with you and will be in you."

This path to intimacy is only traversable by those who are empowered with the Holy Spirit. Jesus knew that without the Spirit to help us navigate the terrain of the narrow way, we would surely misstep and leave the path. In John 14:26 Jesus promised, "The Helper, the Holy Spirit, whom the Father will send in my name, he will teach you all things and bring to your remembrance all that I have said to you."

The Greek word that Jesus uses for the Holy Spirit is *parakletos*, which means one who is summoned to one's side, called to one's aid, one who encourages and comforts.[xii] In other words, Jesus is telling us that as we walk down this path, a helper will come alongside of us to our aid. Not only will he be there, he will encourage us to not deviate from the course of life and will comfort us in our weariness from the spiritual attacks we encounter along this way.

The Way

The first believers in Christ understood that a relationship with God was found through this narrow way. It made perfect sense for Jesus to send the Holy Spirit as a helper for the journey of pursuing God. It actually made so much sense that they adopted the term "The Way" as a name for the church.

Their line of reason is really quite sound. Jesus said, "I am the way, and the truth, and the life. No one comes to the Father except through me" (John 14:6). Therefore, the means by which we connect with God is (to use David's language) by traveling the path of his instruction. This results in a relational intimacy with our Creator. So the early church took upon themselves the name "The Way" because they were following Christ as they traveled on the path to life.

Upon this path they experienced all the difficulties that Jesus foretold. The first believers were persecuted because their path stood in opposition to the path of the religious leaders. This new way was seen as heresy because it challenged the path that the Pharisees taught as the way to God. The most zealous Pharisee, Saul (later to be converted as

Paul), worked tirelessly to bring these early Christians to trial in Jerusalem (see Acts 9:2).

The way of Christ brought people into the kingdom, but it also set them on a collision course with the religious system and its spiritual bondage. Jesus said to them, "But woe to you, scribes and Pharisees, hypocrites! For you shut the kingdom of heaven in people's faces. For you neither enter yourselves nor allow those how would enter to go in" (Matthew 23:13). Nevertheless, the persecution of "The Way" actually fueled the passion of the early church and resulted in countless numbers discovering true supernatural life in the way of Christ.

I'm Coming Your Way

Although the history of this path is interesting, some of you are beginning to wonder, "What does this have to do with creating an *altared* culture of worship?" The purpose behind this history lesson is to, first, enlighten us that there is indeed a path to intimacy with God, and second, to show the need for this way in the culture of our current generation. The idea of a path has not been lost with ancient history; rather, it continues to be a very present and important component of our worship relationship with Christ.

An *altared* culture is discovered upon this path. Like David, we must travel the narrow, often difficult, path through the conduit of God's commands and instruction. This is the only way to experience God in the manner he intended.

Allow me to take it a step further. When we approach God, we must follow the way and words of Jesus. In essence, our proclamation becomes, "Where you go, I go. What you say, I say." The cry of our heart becomes, "I'm coming your way."

With everything in our being we should run after God in reckless abandon. We have access to God through Jesus' death and resurrection! Not only are we vindicated, but we are actually invited to commune with God in his throne room. Hebrews 4:15-16 states, "For we do not have a high priest who is unable to sympathize with our weaknesses but one who in every respect has been tempted as we are, yet without sin. Let us then with confidence draw near to the throne of grace, that we may receive mercy and find grace to help in time of need."

In other words, when we travel the narrow path, we can be confident in the fellowship we have with Christ…because he too traveled this very path. Not only does he "get" what we go through, he is also near to us on our journey. James instructs us to "draw near to God, and he will draw near to you" (James 4:8).

Along this path is where we encounter God. It is impossible to connect with God except by way of Christ. On this path we discover that Jesus is the *way* that we travel, the Holy Spirit is the *helper* in our travels, and God is drawing near to *us* as we journey near to *him*.

Remember, worship is not confined to an event or a song. Worship is actually a conglomeration of events that compose the journey of our lives. Those who take part in this culture understand that a difficult step is as much an act of worship as a step filled with elation. Jesus even told us that most of the steps on this path would be difficult because it's narrow, not wide! "In the world you will have tribulation. But take heart; I have overcome the world" (John 16:33).

I'm Coming My Way

Many Christians find it hard to worship when life is not going as planned. Or when experiencing something they find "unfair." Was it *fair* for the One who never sinned to take upon himself the punishment for our imperfections (see Isaiah 53:1-9)? Was it *right* for the Son of God to be born in a feed trough (see Luke 2:7) and have no place to lay his head (see Matthew 8:20)? I fear that luxury and the comfort of our culture enables many of us to assume we are exempt from the difficulty and discomfort of the way of Christ.

The result of this disassociation is the disengagement on the part of many Christians. When a Christian misunderstands the difficulty of the way of Jesus and replaces it with a softer, more comfortable version, it becomes hard to connect with God, both personally and corporately. We often become angry at God when life is not going according to our dreams and desires. We stop praying and reading God's word. It is retaliation at its finest, an outright attack on God that renders us hopeless, bitter, and empty. In this condition, it is almost impossible to live a life of surrender, which is the evidence of worship (see Romans 12:2).

Such bitterness also makes it burdensome to participate in worship services or in relationships within the church because we are too consumed with our circumstances. Our external pain keeps us from being concerned with God or the needs of others. Forfeiting the opportunity to move towards God, these actions boldly declare, "I'm going my way."

Paul knew this scenario much too well. He reminded us, "Let us consider how to stir up one another to love and good works, not neglecting to meet together, as is the habit of some, but encouraging one another, and all the more as you see the Day drawing near" (Hebrews 10:24-25).

The Day of the Way

There is a day that is drawing near, and it is approaching fast. The day that I am referencing is the day when Jesus returns. On that day no person wants to be associated with something that wears the name of Christ only to discover it is actually the broad and easy way of the world in disguise. When this scenario is true, (which sadly it often is) it serves only to undermine the *altared* culture rather than sustain it. For too long the people that comprise the church have claimed the worship of God, yet their actions are in direct opposition to its message. The world looking in sees the disconnect and as a result rejects the invitation to walk the path of Christ.

The day for real change has arrived. Personal sacrifice in the middle of busyness, confusion and disappointment is what authenticates this worship culture. Any person can praise God joyfully when life is going well. But worship is far more difficult on the narrow path. That is what the world needs to witness...and what God desires from his children.

As we struggle to stay the narrow course, we need to not only be empowered by the Holy Spirit but also by the relationships of others on this way of encountering God. Remember that Paul said we must consider how to stir one another to love and good works? This is crucial because without the relational component, this culture will fail.

We need encouragement from others to love God when we don't desire him. We also need each other to help us remember the past steps of the trek that got us to the place in which we currently stand on the path. The way of intimacy is encompassed by relationship. We were never intended to live alone; we are utterly dependent upon a relationship with God and others.

Eternal life and intimacy with God is not a destination far down the road; it's now! Intimacy is already within us in the form of the Spirit of Christ (see Romans 8:9), and it is ours to be continually experienced and enjoyed along this path. An *altared* culture of worship is the journey we walk through this life.

Culture is impossible without relationships; one person cannot create a culture. We must journey along this path toward Christ collectively and invite others to join the journey. Like culture, intimacy is only experienced in the context of relationship, and along this path both intimacy with God and others is fulfilled.

Restoration

As I stated earlier, the purpose of this path is to restore something that was lost. Genesis 3:8-10 speaks of God walking

The Path to Intimacy

through the garden in the cool of the evening. After the sin of Adam and Eve thwarted their relationship with God, they became ashamed to walk with God. They became aware of God's holiness and their own guilt. Ever since that day, God has been in the process of restoring us to walk with him.

Notice that Jesus was known as Immanuel (see Matthew 1:23), which literally means that God was "with us" in the form of Jesus Christ. He actually came to walk among us. While doing so, he set an example to follow, a way to connect with God. That connection was established through Jesus, and he invites us to walk that same narrow path with him.

Those who live a life of authentic worship on the difficult path and finish well will also be invited to walk with God in the future. In the book of Revelation Jesus spoke of this type of people in the church of Sardis. Jesus described them as "people who have not soiled their garments...they will walk with me in white, for they are worthy" (Revelation 3:4b).

John also spoke of a day when all the redeemed will walk in the light of God's glory. In the New Jerusalem (a picture of heaven), John exclaimed, "And I saw no temple in the city, for its temple is the Lord God, the Almighty and the Lamb. And the city has no need of sun or moon to shine on it, for the glory of God gives it light, and its lamp is the lamb. By its light will the nations walk" (Revelation 21:22-24a).

In other words, God is restoring us so we can one day walk in his unfiltered presence. The great thing is that we can also experience his presence on the narrow path in this life. And this intimate presence he offers us becomes the incubator in which a worship culture thrives. Our movement toward God always flows out of a heart of submission, which in its very essence is worship.

Application

So what path have you been walking? It's easy to assume that our current path is the right one, yet many Christians are unknowingly walking the broad, easy path of the world. Could it be that the reason you are not experiencing the intimacy you desire is because you are not following the way of his instruction?

I encourage you to ponder the steps of your path over the past few years. If your path is leading to destruction, stop and change your course. If you are walking the narrow path, what did each step look like along the journey? Ask God to show you the places he came to your side. Reflect back and realize that each step, easy or difficult, on the path established by Christ was an act of worship.

If you have found yourself complaining along this expedition, simply ask for God's forgiveness and acknowledge that the way of Jesus will often be difficult. The journey is difficult, the path is not easy, but each step shapes you more and more into the worshiper God destines you to be.

Finally, take the next step. Make a declaration that you are coming his way, that you want to go where he goes and lead others to do the same. Once you make this bold proclamation, you are firmly on your way to establishing an *altared* culture of worship in your life and in the community surrounding you.

Chapter 6

The Secret Whisperer

I am not sure of the exact moment when the thought invaded my consciousness, but I know it has captured my passion for some time: *I want to write a book.*

For years I felt that my passion was downright irrational because of my long-time struggle with grammar and phonics. I have to admit, as a child the spelling bee was my most dreaded event of the whole school year! Inevitably, I was the first or second kid disqualified from the competition due to my inability to spell even the simplest of words.

Unfortunately, my skills never improved throughout my grade school education. Each school play or novel that was read aloud in class was yet another opportunity for failure and embarrassment. However, after my path changed I began to study communication for my undergraduate degree, and something shifted. I began to speak publicly and communicate in a variety of ways, including writing.

After graduating with the highest honors my department could award, I still felt that I lacked the ability to clearly communicate my heart through the written word. Despite these inner hurdles, I continued to write as I worked through my graduate degree in worship leadership. It was during those long hours, pouring over biblical texts and developing my theology of worship, that God unleashed a passion for writing. I believe it suits my personality well because writing allows me to ponder and carefully think through the meaning of each individual word.

Although I received good marks on my papers, I still doubted myself and was held captive under the tyranny of my own fear. I really believed I had nothing significant to say and thought myself incapable of completing such a task. It wasn't until I heard God's gentle whisper in the quiet place that I began to move on writing this book.

His gentle but unrelenting call to me was to move forward with my passion and help people create an *altared* culture of worship. Even after I felt sure of the call, I was reluctant and scared. It wasn't until I heard and experienced God personally that I began the process of creating this culture within my church. I began to gather the biblical components and individual stories that would establish the foundation of an *altared* culture.

Interdependent Worship

Most of the book thus far has been centered upon the individual life of worship. The reason for this strong emphasis is that our generation has failed to understand what it really means to create and live within a worship culture for the ninety-nine percent of our lives that is not a church worship service. It's not that I devalue the corporate aspect of worship; after all, my main job is to lead the body of Christ collectively to worship and experience his presence.

I would venture to guess that a large majority of you reading this book have a passion for worship and that you love extended times of corporate gathering among the body of believers. It is my purpose in this chapter to explain the interconnecting and interdependent relationship between those beloved times of corporate worship and the individual outpouring of worship that occurs on a daily basis.

The Undisclosed Place

Throughout his life, Jesus regularly escaped to an undisclosed place to experience a truly personal relationship with his Father. He repeatedly and without explanation left masses of people after they had gathered to hear his teaching, left those wanting to experience the miracle of his healing touch. We might consider it downright selfish and rude for him to so flippantly excuse himself from ministry to retire to these secret places. After all, what *was* he doing on the mountain-top by himself, and why *did* he set out in a boat to get away from the people?

Scripture says that his main purpose was to speak with and worship his Father. Mark makes the following observation of Jesus' practice, "And rising very early morning while it was still dark he departed and went out to a desolate place and there he prayed" (Mark 1:35).

Most of the time when we discuss Jesus' ministry, we emphasize the corporate aspect where he ministered to his select group of twelve or to the masses. It is important, however, to note that these corporate times of ministry would not be possible if Jesus had neglected his individual worship. I would argue that it is impossible to speak and act on behalf of another when the heart and purpose of the one being emulated is not known intimately. Remember Jesus' words, "Truly, truly, I say to you, the Son can do nothing of his own accord, but only what he sees the Father doing. For whatever the Father does, the Son does likewise. For the Father loves the Son and shows him all that he is doing" (John 5:19-20).

The reason Jesus was able to create an *altared* culture corporately is because he constantly worshiped God individually. He spoke about the interdependent relationship between individual and corporate worship on a mountainside one afternoon. And through this speech we will discover that a culture which overemphasizes public acts of worship has plagued God's people throughout history.

Jesus seems to be obsessed with the secret place. In his instruction of giving to the poor he said, "*Beware of practicing your righteousness before other people in order to be seen by them*, for then you will have no reward from your Father who is in heaven. Thus, when you give to the needy, sound no trumpet before you, as the hypocrites do in the synagogues and in the streets that they may be praised by others. Truly, I say to you, they have received their reward. But, when you give to the needy, do not let your left hand know what your right hand is doing, so that your giving may be in *secret*. And your *Father who sees in secret* will reward you" (Matthew 6:1-4, emphasis mine).

Concerning prayer, Jesus taught, "And when you pray, you must not be like the hypocrites. For they love to stand and pray in the synagogues and at the street corners, that they may be seen by others. Truly, I say to you, they have received their reward. But when you pray, go into your room and shut the door and pray to your Father who is in *secret*. And your *Father who sees in secret* will reward you" (Matthew 6:5-6, emphasis mine).

Finally, about fasting, Jesus warned his followers to "not look gloomy like the hypocrites, for they disfigure their faces so their fasting may be seen by others. Truly I say to you, they have received their reward. But when you fast, anoint your head and wash your face, that your fasting may not be seen by others but by your *Father who is in secret*. And your Father *who sees in secret* will reward you" (Matthew 6:16-18, emphasis mine). In these stories Jesus unearths two different ways to approach God. Let's examine them further.

Publicly Approved

The first method is that of the Pharisees. Now before we begin to expose their faulty approach to God, let me first emphasize that their righteousness was far beyond that of the modern church in terms of outward worship. They fasted twice a week, gave a tenth of everything they owned, gave to the poor, read the Word of God, and could recite the Torah word for word (the first five books of the Hebrew Bible) from memory. Most people today would consider them shining examples of Christ followers for their public acts of worship and their contrast with the world.

So if that is true, what was so incorrect about their approach to God? At its essence, their error was based upon the set of eyes for which they performed. While pursuing God and obeying his commandments, they wrongly sought the gaze and admiration of people around them rather than pleasing the heart of God...*who sees in secret.*

The Pharisees held strongly to the belief that corporate worship within their religious culture made them closer to God. Jesus came on the scene and challenged not only the act, but more importantly, the motive behind their worship. He wanted to expose the approval they desperately sought. He knew that if they didn't get their motive for worship centered and focused on the correct set of eyes, they would never experience the relationship with God to which they had ostensibly devoted their entire lives.

What a tragedy of epic proportion: to devote your entire life to worship God, only to discover you had ultimately failed! Imagine the embarrassment, the disgrace, and the disbelief when they realized that the constant "well done" they heard from the crowd was meaningless. When they realized that they would never hear the "well done" from the One who mattered. Instead of a glorious invitation into God's presence, they would hear the stern words, "Depart from me, I never knew you." What a blunder, what a mistake! What a wasted life of miss-focused worship.

Now let's look at how this method of approaching God shows up in our modern context. Is it easier to pray longer, more eloquent prayers when we are in front of others than when alone? Is it easier to jump up and down and sing praise in the midst of a service, but harder to find our voice to declare his goodness throughout our day?

Don't we get something out of describing our service for the church, our generous gifts, or what we have suffered because of our love for God? Of course we have all been guilty of these mistakes in our own lives. Just this week I read the confession of a fellow worship leader who early in his ministry described how he had struggled to have consistent times of worship offstage.

Just last week my mentor commented on the growing number of worship leaders who sit in the audience disengaged, constantly evaluating the worship happening on stage. In contrast, when they are leading, there seems to be an exciting, passionate act of worship displayed in their songs and emotion. In other words when they get before the public eye, they "turn it on." Throughout my years of leading worship, I have seen this dynamic in worship musicians, in other Christian leaders, and ultimately in myself.

When we "turn it on" in the corporate worship service, I believe that we are coming dangerously close to reproducing the Pharisaical method of worship in our generation. We might gain the respect of our peers and deceptively dupe them into believing we are more spiritual than we know ourselves to be...but in the end we are still performing for the wrong set of eyes.

God Approved

In contrast, Jesus was inviting not only the Pharisee, but us as well, to operate under the observations of another set of eyes. Jesus knew that if we did not intentionally engage the divine audience, we would by default act for the approval of others. Jesus' heart for us is to choose the Father's approval because God's eyes are directed towards the righteous (see Psalm 34:15)...meaning that his blessing and favor is upon those who worship God from their innermost being. He doesn't want us to be deceived into thinking that our outward acts of worship could somehow cover for or negate our lack of individual worship.

Hebrews 4:13 states that, "No creature is hidden from his *sight*, but all are naked and exposed to the *eyes* of him to whom we must give account." Don't be deceived; God cares about the secret thoughts and intentions of our heart. The author of Hebrews addressed this truth when he stated, "For the word of God is living and active, sharper than any two-edged sword, piercing to the division of soul and of spirit, of joints and of marrow, and discerning the thoughts and intentions of the heart" (Hebrews 4:12). The reason this often goes unnoticed and unaddressed within the church is because we are being true to what our eyes naturally focus upon: outward appearance.

1 Samuel 16:7 states, "For the Lord sees not as man sees: man looks on the outward appearance, but the Lord looks on the heart." A first reading of this verse could lead to a measure of confusion if not viewed in the proper context. One might ask, "How am I supposed to prove and display the authenticity of my love for God to others if they only see my outward acts of worship?" The answer to this question is that your purpose in worship is to be justified before God alone. So, if we are only engaged in worship during corporate services and gatherings, we are inescapably focused upon our perception of others and consumed with how they perceive us.

The solution to this predicament is that we must take time to worship individually in the secret, undisclosed place. We should constantly remind ourselves and each other that this is the primary place where God examines the thoughts and the intentions of our heart. It was in this hidden place that King David penned these heartfelt words, "*Search* me, O God, and know my heart! Try me and know my thoughts! And *see* if there be any grievous way in me, and lead me in the way everlasting!" (Psalm 139:23-24).

The same set of eyes that searched David's heart are roaming the landscape of humanity to find one that longs to be justified before God. Scripture says, "The eyes of the Lord run to and fro throughout the whole earth, to show Himself strong on behalf of those whose heart is loyal to Him" (2 Chronicles 16:9 NKJV).

Gaze

It is hard for many to accept the truth that God's eyes are focused on them. This escaped my grasp for most of my life because no one effectively told me that I really was a child of God, that I was a recipient of his unending, all-encompassing, unconditional love! Jesus, on the other hand, knew full well that he was accepted and loved by his Father. We could think that this was due to the fact that he was fully God and man, and that he knew this because he had been with God from the beginning (see John 1:1). While this is true, I think there is another component to consider.

I believe that Jesus was constantly reminded of God's love during the time that he spent alone with his Father. It was during these times that he not only allowed God to search his heart, but he learned to focus his gaze upon what his Father was doing and saying.

It would be totally absurd to suggest that Jesus went away to pray because that was fulfilling his religious duty of having a quiet time with God. No. His motive in getting alone with God was the knowledge that an authentic *corporate* life within culture is impossible without authentic *personal* worship. In other words, Jesus focused his gaze upon what God was doing within culture so he could tangible create it with his own life and actions.

We are called to the same purpose in our generation! Not only do we let God judge the thoughts and intentions of our hearts in the secret place, we likewise are to search out the desires of God's heart. This is the purpose of God's Spirit residing within our bodies: to help us understand the things of God and to have one within us who intentionally focuses upon the secret things of God. This allows us to speak and carry out God's secrets in the world. David, a man after God's heart knew this truth well. He commented, "The secret of the Lord is for those who fear Him, and He will make them know his covenant" (Psalm 25:14). Listen to what Paul says concerning this subject,

> "What no eye has seen, nor ear heard, nor the heart of man imagined, what God has prepared for those who love him"— these things God has revealed to us through the Spirit. For the Spirit searches everything, even the depths of God. For who knows a person's thoughts except the spirit of that person, which is in him? So also no one comprehends the thoughts of God except the Spirit of God. Now we have received not the spirit of the world, but the Spirit who is from God, that we might understand the things freely given us by God. And we impart this in words not taught by human wisdom but taught by the Spirit, interpreting spiritual truths to those who are spiritual" (1 Corinthians 2:9-13).

Secret Eyes

Have you ever been in a room where only you and another person know a secret? The people gathered around you think they are talking about the same thing you are, when in fact, they are a million miles away. As the conversation proceeds, you use furtive glances to catch the eye of the other who knows your secret.

Often a smirk comes over your face as you quickly try to cover the fact that you are "in the know." This is the way that I illustrate Jesus' relationship with his Father...which also portrays our own relationship with God. When we allow the dual searching of hearts that I described earlier, we know and understand God's purposes within our society and within our daily lives. We follow the example of Jesus, who learned to focus his gaze upon God individually, which in turn empowered him to know God's heart and live it out corporately. He is inviting us to participate in the same experience, to be "in the know" with him, every day of our lives.

Corporate Worship

Now that we have stated the importance of individual worship, let's turn our focus back to corporate worship. First, I want to note that Jesus displayed acts of outward worship every day of his ministry as is portrayed in the gospels. He also gathered to worship with others in the temple. So, we can conclude that corporate worship is an important part of our engagement with God.

Throughout Scripture we see an emphasis on the corporate gathering. David proclaimed, "I will tell of your name to my brothers; in the midst of the congregation I will praise you" (Psalm 22:22). There is a section in the book of Psalms (120-134) that is referred to as the "Songs of Ascents;" these were songs that people sang as they were journeying to Jerusalem to celebrate the Passover together.

In the New Testament, just after Jesus ascended into heaven, the disciples gathered corporately and waited for the gift of the Holy Spirit (Acts 2). Not only did they meet together one time for one event, the writer of Hebrews instructed them not to forsake gathering together regularly for the purpose of stirring one another to love and good works (Hebrews 10:25). Finally, Paul repeatedly instructed early believers in Corinth on how to conduct orderly worship (1 Corinthians 14:26-40) and educated the church in Ephesus how to worship God in community (Ephesians 5:19-21).

Because the form of corporate worship received such emphasis in the early church, we need to find its relevance in our modern context. The importance of shared worship in our generation is similar to past generations:

1) It allows individual believers to come together and function as the body of Christ through their Spiritual Gifts (see Romans 12:3-8 & 1 Corinthians 12).
2) It teaches and informs new believers how to connect with God (see 1 Corinthians 14:31-33).
3) It provides a witness to outsiders and unbelievers who are in attendance (see 1 Corinthians 14:24-25).
4) It teaches individuals how to submit in humility to one another out of reverence for Christ (see Ephesians 5:21 and Philippians 2:5-9).
5) It allows us to confess our sins to one another (see James 5:16).
6) It allows us to encourage and comfort one another in the midst of trials (see 2 Corinthians 1:3-5).
7) It spurs us to practice love and good works (see Hebrews 10:24-25).
8) It's a place where we can celebrate and make melody in our hearts to the Lord (see Ephesians 5:19-20 & Colossians 3:16-17.
9) It allows us to hear the Word of God and respond collectively to its commands (see Nehemiah 8:3 and Romans 10:17).
10) It allows us to give a tithe and offering to meet the needs of those in the Body and further the kingdom of God (see Malachi 3:6-12 and Acts 2:45).
11) It gives us a setting where we can pray for each other and for healing (see James 5:14-16).

As you look through this list of amazing things that happen when followers of Christ gather, notice the impact of correct motives. The Pharisees focused on the outward act and neglected their inward motive, which rendered their worship utterly void. Jesus focused on the inward motive of God's heart and lived it out among other believers, which yielded a drastically different result.

The fruit that was born out of his ministry was due to individually abiding in the Vine (his Father, see John 10). The lack of fruit that was displayed in the Pharisees' lives (whom Jesus referred to as whitewashed tombs) shows the effect of outward acts without inward relationship. The same can be true of our outward acts of worship today if we do not walk with and experience God in the undisclosed place.

Incorporating Worship into Culture

The final thing I would like to discuss in this chapter is the fact that Jesus not only worshiped individually and corporately, but he also incorporated worship into his culture. Jesus not only lived out his worship in the temple courts, he also incorporated it into the culture that surrounded him, sometimes even in forbidden places.

We find him in taboo Samaritan villages, touching lepers, and connecting with social outcasts—tax collectors, prostitutes, and uneducated fisherman—all of whom would have been rejected in their day. Jesus had the ability to display a life of worship because he had been empowered individually and reminded corporately of God's purpose, which enabled him to see what God was doing and hear what God was saying within the culture of his day. Because of this, he created an *altared* culture that led others to worship God, a culture that has shaken the world ever since.

Jesus introduced to his society a new way of living which radically changed people's perceptions and altered the way they related to God. Don't you think if we are created in his image, we are supposed to be about the same business? God has called both you and me to create something that most of the world cannot perceive. If we want to impact, we have to create. When we initiate worship from the inward secret place, it naturally leads to corporate acts of worship that are authentic, not fake, which in turn allows us to live something out that the world has never seen before!

My own creative effort in this book is the overflow of time spent in the secret place. It was not until God whispered to me individually that I had the confidence to bring this book idea to the body of Christ. Because of an inward whisper, I was able to bring an outward act of worship (my writing) before you...not for your approval, but to worship God with the talent he gave me. Now, and only now, will I be able to create this culture within my society that I have longed to see.

Application

As you have read this chapter, it is possible you have realized that, one, your outward acts of worship are not built upon a foundation of inward worship, or that two, your outward acts of worship are not empowering you to create an *altared* culture around you. Both scenarios ultimately result in ineffectiveness because neither are God's best for our lives.

You are not alone in either situation; I believe a majority of us have found ourselves there at one point or another in our lives. I suggest you start fresh today. Follow Jesus' example of finding and fighting to protect that secret undisclosed place in your life. After you have identified that space, nourish yourself with it daily.

Once you have established this place, you will become very dependent on it, which is a sign that you are beginning to replicate Jesus' example. Pay close attention to what God whispers to you in that place. You will then have the ability to authentically act it out corporately for his eyes only and will possess the confidence to incorporate it into the culture you are creating within society!

Section 3
The Path to a New Culture

Chapter 7

Milepost 1: Let Go, Let Loose

"What Was That All About?"

I could not believe it, I was late again. I threw my guitar on my back, grabbed my music, and ran out the door. I was scheduled to play in an 8:30am service, and it was already 8:15am. And the church building was over ten minutes away.

By this time in my life I had fulfilled my promise to God to serve him one hundred percent, and the means to serving him right now was by leading worship. I had been obedient with a rather large component of my life, which felt liberating, but also left me with anxious fears of what the future would hold. To the best of my knowledge I had begun to follow Jesus' example of dependency, desperation, and obedience. *Now put that thought on hold.*

As I ran to the driveway to jump into my truck, I realized that it had rained...and it just so happens that we had not had rain in about a month. I was a little frustrated because I knew I was going to have to wash my truck, which at the time was my most valued possession. Now, I had given up my career in Motorsports Engineering, but I had not given up my love for going fast and owning fast cars. So down the road I went like a bat out of hell hoping to make it there in time. Being late also gave me a great excuse to go fast and test my limits a little on the way.

I headed down one of the most challenging roads on my route to church and came upon my favorite curve. It was almost a ninety degree banking turn that sloped downhill. I

Milepost 1: Let Go, Let Loose

had a goal of tackling the turn at a high rate of speed, sliding the back of the truck sideways on the wet road and continuing on in my journey. I threw the truck into third gear at fifty miles per hour so I could spin the tires.

Everything was going as planned, but I lost control. As I headed toward the bank I knew it was not going to be good. My truck impacted the bank at just the right angle to roll my truck down the downhill slope. My truck was destroyed, my stuff was thrown out the windows, and I had glass all over me. I regained my thoughts and asked myself, "What was that all about?"

Characteristics of a Worship Culture

You may have noticed that I have not mentioned music and worship services much in this book so far. And you may find that puzzling. After all, this book is supposed to be about how to create culture of worship, right? And this is true, but we must first discuss the foundation and principles of the culture before we can talk about the by-product of the culture. Hang in there with me and really dig deep within your soul to excavate God's desire for worship. Could it be that God us calling us to worship more than through just a song or a service?

The first section of this book has been devoted to Jesus' example as the number one worshiper. He said and did only what he heard his father saying and doing, he satisfied his hunger and thirst in doing the will of his father, and finally, he had a fear of God which resulted in intimacy. Or we could summarize by saying that Jesus modeled dependency, desperation, and obedience. The second section of the book identified the beginning steps of this journey to create a culture. Now we are unpacking major components of an *altared* culture that are built upon this framework and establishing the characteristics that define it. As we follow Jesus' example of worship, we will discover there are natural byproducts that will be displayed in our lives. The first milepost on our journey is brokenness.

Transformation

In previous chapters we have referenced the idea of transformation. We sifted through verses that described the transformation from what we were to what we are becoming, basically a new identity. 2 Corinthians 3:18 says, "We all, with unveiled face, beholding the glory of the Lord, are being transformed into the same image from one degree of glory to another. For this comes from the Lord who is the Spirit." Romans 12:2 says, "Do not be conformed to this world, but be transformed by the renewal of your mind that by testing you may discern what is the will of God, what is good and acceptable and perfect."

These verses sound good, but what do they mean? How in the world are we supposed to be transformed, and how is God doing it in us? There are various ways that the Lord changes us, but one main method the Lord uses in our lives is brokenness. Most of us don't like to hear that word because it brings up images of pain and feelings of apprehension. Let's press through those barriers to uncover God's idea of brokenness.

Brokenness

One of the first principles we need to understand in the transformative journey toward worshippers is brokenness of the outer man. I know you are probably asking yourself, "What is the outer man?" In this section I am going to use some ideas and phrases from my favorite author, Watchman Nee. He describes the subject of the inward and outward man in this way.

Milepost 1: Let Go, Let Loose

> "When God comes to indwell us by His Spirit with His life and power, He comes into our spirit at the time when we were born again (John 3:6). The regenerated spirit located at the center of man's being is what we call the inward man. Secondly, outside the sphere of this inward man indwelt by God is the soul. Its functions are our thoughts, emotions, and will. We thus will speak of the spirit as the inward man, the soul as the outer man."[xiii]

Now that we have made the distinction between the inward and outward man, let's look at its implications on worship. Let me illustrate the struggle between the inward and outward man in words that I think we can all identify with. Let's look at Paul's writing to the Roman church.

> "I do not understand my own actions. For I do not do what I want, but I do the very thing I hate. Now if I do what I do not want, I agree with the law, that it is good. So now it is no longer I who do it, but sin that dwells within me. For I know that nothing good dwells in me, that is in my flesh [*outward man*]. For I have the desire to do what is right [*inward man*], but not the ability to carry it out [*outward man*]. For I do not do the good I want [*inward man*], but the evil I do not want is what I keep on doing [*outward man*]. Now if I do what I do not, it is no longer I who do it, but sin that dwells within me." (Romans 7:15-20)

Paul is explaining what many of us feel every day of our lives. We accept Jesus' rule and reign in our lives, and we surrender our allegiance to Him alone. His Spirit takes up residence in our spirit. The Holy Spirit gives us the mind and the heart of Jesus (see 1 Corinthians 2:16). Therefore, we desire the things that he desires. However, there is another mindset that stands opposed to God. God still has to reckon with and deal with our own will before we can be utterly dependent upon him, which is authentic worship.

How does God break the outward man? Well, there are three different ways in which he normally works within the life of an individual. For some people the breaking is sudden, for some it is gradual, and for others God uses a sudden breaking, followed by gradual work to form them into worshipers.

God uses our daily trials and circumstances of life to break the outward man in us. He does this, not with the intention of harming us, but so we can experience a greater intimacy with him. Which is worship. We must allow the cross of Christ to break our outer man. Nee describes that mysterious transformation this way: "The cross reduces the outward man to death. It splits open the human shell. The cross must break all that belongs to our outward man – our opinions, our ways, our cleverness, our self-love, our selfish interest, our all."xiv

Alone in the Woods

Now, I would not say that I arrived at that the place of complete death of the outward man in my life, but I have had many incidences in my life that have inched me closer to that goal. One of those days was early on in seminary. Lots of people have terrible things to say about seminary, but there are many valuable things that happen in a person life while they set apart time to study about God.

On this particular day I was sitting in an evangelism class with about fifty or sixty in attendance. The professor requested that about five or six students stand up, so a few brave souls heeded the call and timidly rose from their seat, anxiously awaiting what was coming next. The silence was

Milepost 1: Let Go, Let Loose

deafening as the professor looked over the crowd. After the a few moments he stated, "If statistics are correct, this will be all that is left of you by the end of your ministry. Some will leave due to burnout, hurt, and bad leadership decisions. Others will commit adultery, misuse finances in the church, or allow their pride to destroy everything they hold dear."

I remember sitting in the crowd thinking that I would never be one of those people as I scanned the classroom wondering which classmate would be the first to fall prey to the professor's words. I had resolved to stand strong because of my zeal to worship God and live a life that honored him. To my amazement the professor then looked over the class and said words that cut to the core of my being and exposed something I had not yet discovered. He said, "If you are sitting in your chair and you are thinking that this could never happen to you, you will be the first to go." My pride lay bare before my very eyes, and for the first time I realized that it must be broken for me to finish well.

That weekend I went and walked through the woods and prayed for hours. I got down on my knees, crying and surrendering every part of my outward man to God. I asked him to deal with my flesh and fill me with his Spirit so I might finish the race well and lead others to do the same. My outward man had to be broken and dealt with before I could ever truly worship God.

Importance of Brokenness

The reason this is such a key component to worship is that *we don't actually worship*. No, I haven't gone crazy, just try to follow my line of thinking. No person can come to God unless he has enabled them, Jesus says in John 6:65. Second, no one can claim or confess that Christ is Lord over their life except by the power of the Holy Spirit (see 1 Corinthians 12:3). Third, the Spirit of God lives freely in every believer, which allows us to cry "Abba (daddy) Father" and experience the intimacy God intends for us (see Romans 8:15-16). Finally, the Spirit intercedes on our behalf according to the will of God (see Romans 8:26-27). That's why it is not us doing the worshipping!

In other words, God's purpose for brokenness in our lives is to release the Holy Spirit inside us to worship the way that God intends. Scripture says, "Do you not know that your body is a temple of the Holy Spirit within you, whom you have from God? You are not your own, for you were bought with a price. So glorify God in your body" (1 Corinthians 6:19-20). If this true, transformational brokenness allows our outward man to be broken in order to give room for the Spirit of God to be released in our inner man. And obviously, "man" in this sense includes both women and men.

Release

In a previous chapter I stated that John 4:24 can be rather confusing: "God is spirit, and those who worship him must worship in spirit and truth." Although there are several interpretations of what this means, if you look at the passage in this context I believe Jesus is addressing our inward man (the human spirit) when he calls us to worship in spirit and truth. In other words, if we are to worship correctly, there must be a release of both our spirits [the inward man] and the Holy Spirit that resides in us. Nee explains this relationship in this way,

> "When we received our new spirit through regeneration, simultaneously we also received God's Spirit. The moment our human spirit is raised from the state of death, we receive the Holy Spirit. We often say that the Holy Spirit and our spirit have become joined together. While each is uniquely separate, they nevertheless are not so easily distinguishable.

Milepost 1: Let Go, Let Loose

> Thus, the release of the spirit is the release of both the human spirit as well as the Divine Spirit, who resides in the spirit of man."[xv]

In this passage of John, Jesus is calling us to worship from our inward man, without interference from our outward man, which is weighed down by our own selfish desires. God is inviting us to learn through our brokenness that he is releasing his Spirit to worship on our behalf...and this frees our own spirit to engage with him. This progression always results in life and intimacy.

Remember, worship is following Jesus' example of saying and doing what the Father prompts within each moment. If we are engaged with God by allowing him to break our outward man, we experience God in the same way. If not, we are continually frustrated with an inward desire to worship and outward resistance to engage.

Have you ever noticed how difficult it can be to surrender your own will to God? It is easy for most of us to come to God with our agenda and our conditions: "God, if you will do this, I will do this in return." "God, let your will be done in my life, but here is the way I think you should answer my request." This line of thinking is not worship at all. The bondage of our own willfulness is what Jesus was trying to set us free from. In other words, Jesus is saying to us, "Let go, let loose of yourself and your opinions."

Don't be fooled, "It is not passivity; it is a most active life, trusting the Lord like that; drawing life from him, taking him to be our very life, letting him live his life in us as we go forth in his Name."[xvi] Jesus' example of doing and saying what his Father desired was an invitation and challenge for us to live the same. Remember, he told the disciples that he had food that they knew nothing about (see John 4:31). He knew of a satisfaction, a source that fulfilled the longings and desires of his spirit, and it was God himself. Our act of worship should be exactly the same.

The Path to a New Culture

Not many people have arrived at this surrender and satisfaction, myself included, but that does not mean it is not obtainable. When God's Spirit is released in us, worship will take on a new meaning. We will do and say things we never thought we could. Love for God and his purposes will consume our every thought, not because we desire it, but because his Spirit is released to pour out worship and expand this culture in our relationships, family, community, and church.

The Accident

God spoke clearly to me the day of my truck accident. "Eric, I want all of you and all of your affection." I knew God was breaking me, and I responded, "God, I have given you my career, my aspirations, and my dreams. But now you can be Lord over every single part of my life. I'm broken and I am tired of trying to make life work without you." That was a life-altering day for me! That day God began to teach me that my outward man would only hinder my true desire to worship.

What about you? Is there something in your life that God has been doing for some time that you have tried to avoid? Are you trying to make sense of a sudden event that has left you asking, "Why?" It could be that God is in the process of breaking you too, transforming you into a true worshipper. It could be that the outward man is almost gone, and you are getting ready to really worship in the way your heart has longed for so long. Now it's your turn to respond to God's voice.

Alabaster Flask

The beauty of brokenness is illustrated in the following story of worship. "And while he was at Bethany in the house of Simon the leper, as he was reclining at table, a woman came with an alabaster flask of ointment of pure nard, very costly, and she broke the flask and poured it over his head" (Mark

14:3). Jesus responded to the accusations in the room, "Leave her alone. Why do you trouble her? She has done a beautiful thing to me" (Mark 14:6).

> "If the alabaster box is not broken, the pure nard will not flow forth. Strange to say, many are still treasuring the alabaster box, thinking that its value exceeds that of the ointment. Many think that their outward man is more precious than their inward man. Without the breaking of the outward, the inward fragrance will not come forth. Why then should we hold our outward man to be so precious, especially if the outward only contains the fragrance, instead of releasing the fragrance?"[xvii]

What a beautiful picture of worship! Listen to God's plan for your life of worship as you read the following passage. Notice that this worship is not contained to a service, a place, or time. Once a fragrance is released, it is nearly impossible for one to contain its scent. "But thanks be to God, who in Christ always leads us in triumphal procession, and through us spreads the fragrance of the knowledge of him everywhere. For we are the aroma of Christ to God among those who are being saved and among those who are perishing" (2 Corinthians 2:14-15). Let the fragrance of your inward spirit engage in worship and intimacy with the God who created you. When this happens, we create a new culture of worship that leads those who are perishing closer to the One who gave his life to save them.

Application

I invite you to dig into some places that might be a little uncomfortable as you unearth some of these circumstances in your life. First make this distinction: God does not make sinful things happen in your life. We live in a fallen world where sin is the norm, not the exception. God's purpose for arranging our circumstances is always to give us life, not destroy it. Jesus came so we can have life more abundantly, but Satan always comes to steal, kill, and destroy (see John 10:10).

I encourage you to write down some things that have been going on in your life that you have questions about. It could be poor evaluations at work, an unexplained event, or seemingly impossible odds mounting against you. There is an unlimited list of possibilities. As you compile your list, simply ask, "God, were you trying to break something in me when _____ happened?" Pause and listen.

Repeat this over and over as you go through your list. If you don't hear anything, just be patient and keep seeking. The answers will come to you over time. I firmly believe that you will know the answer if you really search God's heart and your own inward man on these topics.

You may find pride, self-sufficiency, or a rebellious nature. God will begin to open your eyes to reveal how he has been working through the years in your life. When he does, simply submit—which is your act of worship—and invite him to bring the breaking to completion so you can be the true person (worshiper) he created you to be. On to the next milepost!

Chapter 8

Milepost 2: The Anchor of Identity

He glanced down in disbelief, then lifted his eyes and stared at me. I felt like his eyes were lasers, cutting right through my soul, and his non-verbals screamed, "Are you serious?" The situation was going south with every passing second as sweat began to run down my back and my hands grew clammy.

As you can tell, I was more than a little nervous: A lot was on the line for me that day. What could possibly generate this kind of stress? A promotion at work? My last meeting with my department chair to certify graduation? No. It was actually far more serious than those seemingly trivial situations. The issue on this particular day centered upon my very identity. How did it come to that?

I was visiting friends and mission church planters in Hamburg, Germany. There is a large population of international students in Hamburg, but the presence of the Christian church was all but non-existent there. Yet God was clear when he placed this region and these people upon my heart, and I went to help wherever I was needed. I had a great time sharing the gospel on college campuses, prayer walking, and encouraging the few believers who were present.

By the end of the trip I was running out of clean clothes, but fortunately, the people with whom I was staying had a washing machine and dryer. I was excited about traveling home with fresh jeans and shirt and started to empty pockets before tossing everything in. And in my haste, I somehow overlooked one important thing. My passport! I left it in a pair of jeans and as you have probably already deduced, it came out in a nice little shriveled ball with an indiscernible picture.

I walked nervously through the airport on that significant final day of my trip, not knowing if the customs office would accept this pitiful document and let me board the plane. After all, who would believe it was me? My identity had been destroyed.

Identity Theft

In the world in which we live, we constantly hear of individuals who have had a vast array of personal information vanish in a second because of identity theft. And because of that, we only order from secure websites and are constantly looking over our virtual shoulder. We are subsequently bombarded by an advertising culture who preys upon our insecurity. "They" promise to protect our identity from the mythical thief who is waiting to steal our individuality.

Why is this scary? Because we are taught by that same culture to make a name for ourselves, to work hard and prove to the world that our name is valid. Our identity is essential to our very being and existence in our world. Without it, we are lost. The second milepost on our journey to create an *altared* culture of worship is identity.

From the beginning of time, the people of God have struggled with their identity. Moses did not believe that he was able to lead God's people out of Egypt (see Exodus 3:11). Jeremiah looked down upon himself because of his youth and his disbelief that God's people would listen to him (see Jeremiah 1:6). Gideon did not believe that he would be able to lead Israel in battle because of his perceived weakness, despite God's assurance of victory (see Judges 6:14-15). Elijah struggled with his identity, doubting that God would protect him after he destroyed all the false prophets of Baal, called down fire from heaven, and started and ended a drought (see 1 Kings 19:9-10). I am not suggesting that the ideology of identity doesn't matter; on the contrary, I want to affirm that this is the way God created us and that identity is a key component in the development of the *altared* culture.

Identity in Worship

In the previous chapter, I shared the concept of release: that God is breaking our outward man with the intention of releasing his Spirit through our inward man. This is important because we must realize that through tough circumstances and hardships, God is breaking us in order to birth authentic worship in us. Without this breaking, the Holy Spirit, which longs to worship God (see Romans 8:15), is never given place to lead us to become the worshipers that God intends us to be. The reason our identity must be solidified and understood is because we worship based upon how we perceive ourselves.

Hang in there with me. This is not narcissistic thinking! I'm talking about taking hold of the kind of worship God most desires through a *selfless* identity. Remember, we stated earlier that worship is engaging with God. Satan, on the other hand, wants us to disengage with God. This leads to self-worship and always ends in our death and destruction. The only way to combat this destructive self-worship is for us to discover and own our new identity in Christ.

2 Corinthians 5:17 says, "Therefore, if anyone is in Christ, he is a new creation. The old has passed away; behold, the new has come." My concern is that most of us have not discovered our true identities. Paul reminded the believers at the Colossian church, "You have put off the old self with its practices and have put on the new self, which is being renewed in the knowledge after the image of its creator" (Colossians 3:9-10). Many Christians become disengaged within their personal relationship with Christ, the church, and their family because of a lack of revelation in this area.

Proverbs 29:18 states, "Where there is no revelation, the people cast off restraint." The word *restraint* is from the

Hebrew word *para* which can mean *"to let go, let loose, or ignore."* In other words, a person or group of people who do not know their identity and are not living off the words that come from God (see Matthew 4:4) are disengaged with their new creation, ignore their true calling, and let themselves go without restraint.

This loss of identity disables individuals from discovering their God-given self. Christians who refuse to "restrain" themselves and engage their new creation exemplify dangerously similar behaviors to those scripture identifies as the individuals who do not know God at all. They have cut themselves loose from God, they have let go of their moorings and now ignore the object of their true worship; instead they worship themselves, their false ideals, and the material possessions of this world (see Romans 1:21-23).

Participatory Worship

One of the visible signs of a healthy culture of worship is participation. Participation can be visible displays of affection or it can be ways in which we relationally engage with God. Although most of us desire to live and operate in such a culture, we are surrounded by those who stand in opposition.

We have all seen it: the people who stand in a service with their arms crossed, lips tightly shut, and apparent disgust on their face. It seems as though they will die if forced to sit through one more minute of this unbearable event. Not only is it seen in worship services, it can also be spotted in relationships. It is often seen in a family unit where the individual members disengage from one another, inevitably leaving each detached and isolated.

We see it within the church family as well. Someone is struggling with sin, somebody has offended them, and they leave the fellowship of the church to be alone. Let's face it—disengagement surrounds every aspect of our lives. In the church many choose not to participate because they have an incorrect view of worship; they have never experienced an authentic worship relationship with God or been taught how to function within a healthy culture of worship. Yet God invites us to participate and be fully engaged, not only in a worship service but in every aspect of our lives. He created us to experience him and his creation intimately and abundantly (see John 10:10b).

The Enemy of Worship

People who are disengaged with God are often oppressed by what I call the "enemy of worship." The enemy of worship is not Satan himself, but it is rooted in his lies and deception. The enemy of worship is our own self-reliance. And self-reliance is based upon the foundation of a wrong identity. A false identity either leads people to worship the incorrect thing, or it causes them to approach God incorrectly. Let me illustrate this through my own life.

For years I approached God as "dirty rotten." I sometimes referred to myself as a dirty, rotten sinner...with condemnation, guilt, and disgrace weighing heavily upon my shoulders. My worship of God was filtered through my own shortcomings and habitual failures as a Christian. I honestly thought God was continually mad at me, and I fully expected him to end my life prematurely because of the disappointment that I must be to him. Sounds pretty dismal, doesn't it?

Well guess what? I was not alone. Many of you reading this book actually struggle with the same issues, even though you may not have ventured out into the uncharted waters of vulnerability to verbalize such dreadful thoughts. Don't worry, it's okay! The purpose of addressing the enemy of worship is to defeat it...which frees us to worship God in the life-giving way he always intended.

My personal problem was that I was relying upon myself to produce righteousness, to be good enough to make God happy. You often hear people say, "I hope I've been good enough to get into heaven." Non-Christians often say it and, even though Christians don't say it, they often believe it due to a flawed understanding of their identity. They are living, just as I was, out of their old identity instead of their new one!

Your new identity is rooted in the reality of ownership. The self-reliant person still falsely believes that they are in control of their life. The worshiper, on the other hand, knows that he or she is not their own; that they have been purchased by God. 1 Corinthians 6:19-20 says, "Do you not know that your body is a temple of the Holy Spirit within you, whom you have from God? You are not your own, for you were bought with a price. So glorify God in your body." In other words, we worship and glorify God by our very existence…if we are living out of our new identity.

On this subject Watchman Nee comments, "How good it is to have the consciousness that we belong to the Lord and we are not our own. There is nothing more precious in the world. It is that which brings the awareness of his continual presence, and the reason is obvious. I must first have the sense of God's possession of me before I can have the sense of his presence with me."[xviii] You often hear people say that they don't experience the presence of God as much as they wish. Do you think there is a correlation here?

Is it possible that people don't experience the presence of God because they don't fully understand the concept of reliance upon God rather than upon themselves? There is nothing more beautiful than a worshipper rooted in an identity of complete reliance upon God. On the other hand, the person who does not understand this truth is held in bondage by the enemy of worship.

In my own life I battled for my identity because I knew the Spirit of God was calling me to live in total reliance upon God, but I still desired to make all the tough decisions of my life. I was convinced that I had to obtain holiness by my own righteous acts. I would not have stated it in those terms verbally, but I lived my life with an overwhelming pressure to

Milepost 2: The Anchor of Identity

perform. When I completed an act that I thought would gain God's approval, I felt close to him, righteous, often boasting of my accomplishment. On the other hand, if I committed a sin, I believed God could never love me. I would painstakingly try to work harder to rack up enough good things to outweigh the bad.

All the while in my striving to please God with my service for him I was further alienating myself from the One who had already clothed me in righteousness. Sure, I knew that heaven was the product of Jesus' sacrifice, but I was quite content to labor in order to earn his favor. I wanted him to like me and love me, but I was enslaved by the enemy of a false identity that inevitably left me disengaged from the One I was striving so hard to please.

People whom the enemy has held in bondage are able to function within a culture of worship, but they are inevitably left with a life of contradiction. Even though they genuinely love God and want to praise him, they are still reliant upon themselves. They go throughout their day preoccupied with their own agenda, not stopping to think and ask, "God, what would you have me do today?" or "God, would you give me your power today to help me live for and worship you?"

People who are enslaved by the false identity of self-reliance find it difficult to pray, difficult to connect with God, and difficult to participate in worship both private and corporate. When they actually do lift their eyes from themselves, it's really hard for them to say, "God, I desperately need you."

The reason it is so difficult is that they really don't need God (or so they display in their actions). They believe in him intellectually, but their hearts have not made the connection. Thus, they spend most of life functioning in their own power and strength. When a self-reliant person comes into the church to worship, they often find it difficult to engage, to cry out in praise and desperation: "All I need is You. You alone satisfy me!"

Why? Because it is a lie. And they know it's hypocritical to sing those words, so they either choose not to participate or they disengage. Remember, we approach God with hunger and desperation because this is the model that Jesus displayed for us to follow. Jesus was always engaged in his relationship with God and with others. The enemy of worship is directly opposed to this constant engagement. **Self-reliance always deceptively coerces the individuals to focus inward, feeding the selfish desires of the flesh and leads us to disengagement instead of allowing the Spirit to lead us to the worship Jesus modeled.**

Paul reminded the Christians in Rome of their identity battle when he said,

> "But if God himself has taken up residence in your life, you can hardly be thinking more of yourself than of him. Anyone, of course, who has not welcomed this invisible but clearly present God, the Spirit of Christ, won't know what we're talking about. But for you who welcome him, in whom he dwells—even though you still experience all the limitations of sin—you yourself experience life on God's terms. It stands to reason, doesn't it, that if the alive-and-present God who raised Jesus from the dead moves into your life, he'll do the same thing in you that he did in Jesus, bringing you alive to himself? When God lives and breathes in you (and he does, as surely as he did in Jesus), you are delivered from that dead life. With his Spirit living in you, your body will be as alive as Christ's!" (Romans 8:9-11 MSG)

So Christ is actually in us by his Spirit and is enabling us to defeat the enemy of worship. Jesus is giving us a new identity in which we can live and operate. It is only in this new identity that one can truly worship God. Does this make sense?

New Identity

Who are you? That's a good question. Before you answer it, let me ask another one. *Have you ever stopped to ask yourself if your perceived personality is your true identity?* We will come back to that thought in a minute. So, who are you? If we actually went through every verse in Scripture that dealt with your new identity, I could write a book on that subject alone. Instead, I will just hit a few of the major ideas that comprise your new identity.

You are a new creation (see 2 Corinthians 5:17). You are a child of God (see John 1:12, Romans 8:1-16). You are a co-heir with Christ, sharing in his inheritance (see Romans 8:17). Your body is a temple and houses the Holy Spirit (see 1 Corinthians 3:16; 6:19). And you are a saint (see Ephesians 1:18). Paul instructs us, "Put off your old self, which belongs to your former manner of life and is corrupt through deceitful desires, and...be renewed in the spirit of your minds, and...put on the new self, created after the likeness of God in true righteousness and holiness" (Ephesians 4:22-24).

Wow, have you ever thought about yourself that way? I am sure there are a variety of responses to that question. Some of you are amazed that the Bible really says that about your new identity, and you are chomping at the bit to dig in and starting living in your new identity. You have been unaware of these amazing truths that God has crafted for you. Others of you have heard this message for many years and know it intellectually...but you don't live everyday life in this identity. In either case, disengagement has been your norm. Although this has been true in the past, Jesus is inviting all of us into our true identity so we can engage in worship and experience God in a whole new dimension.

There may be some of you who find yourselves resistant to live in this new identity. You find comfort in the way you have been relating to the world and to God. You think it's simpler to handle life on your own because it seems to be in your control. You like control, and the idea of total faith can be overwhelming and downright scary. To that end Watchman Nee states, "God must bring us all to the place where we see that we are utterly weak and helpless."[xix]

Why would God do such as thing? you ask yourself. Remember, God is breaking the outward man by allowing you to see the failure of your own perceived self, not to harm you, but to invite you into an intimacy of worship you have never known. God never minds taking something of lesser value from us in order to give us something better. And his "better" always exceeds our imagination!

New Name, New Claim

Have you ever noticed that God likes to give people new names? He renamed Abram to Abraham (see Genesis 17:5), Sarai to Sarah (see Genesis 17:15), Jacob to Israel (see Genesis 32:28), Simon to Peter (see Matthew 16:17-18) and Saul to Paul (see Acts 13:9). *Why would he do this?* I believe it is because God loves to give us a glimpse of our new identity.

Throughout Scripture, a name defined a man or woman's life. It was their prophetic destiny...and eventually became their legacy. I believe that God knows we will only live into his intended future if he unveils our new identity with a new name. We can only engage and worship with God when we know who we are, what he has done for us, and what he is doing through us. (This is the reason the New Testament is chalk full of our new identity in Christ). God is constantly reminding us, "You are somebody new! Live and relate to me in your new self, which I have placed in you by my Spirit!"

Milepost 2: The Anchor of Identity

Who Am I?

Now let's answer my other question. Have you ever really stopped to ponder your own identity? The normal answer is to start by stating your name, family, occupation, and hobbies. Now don't get me wrong: These are all legitimate things that contribute to your identity. If probed further, we may discuss our personality traits. Some of you would say; "I have a quick temper," "I'm shy," "I hate conflict," or "I am competitive."

Now, let's go really deep for just a moment and unearth some of your *false* identity...so we can sift through the lies and discover the jewels that are hidden within you. What if who you perceive yourself to be is actually false? What if your shyness, your temper, your extroversion, or whatever trait you want to name is not actually who you are at all? Maybe, just maybe, all those characteristics are part of your old self-reliant, outward man and actually cause you to disengage. What then?

Paul claimed, "I have been crucified with Christ, it is no longer I who live, but Christ who lives in me. And the life I now live in the flesh, I live by faith in the Son of God, who loved me and gave himself for me" (Galatians 2:20). Shouldn't this be the same testimony of you and me as worshipers? We no longer live in the false, fleshly identity. We are now new creations, complete with a new identity that allows us to approach God boldly with full assurance of our relationship through Christ!

Who was Jesus and what was his identity? Continually full of the Spirit, his identity was expressed by the fruit of the Spirit: "love, joy, peace, patience, kindness, goodness, faithfulness, gentleness, and self-control" (Galatians 5:22-23a).

Now this is our identity as worshipers because it is the identity of Jesus. When you experience anything contrary to these traits, it is a good sign that you are operating in a falsely-perceived self rather than a God-given identity. God gave you this new identity through Christ and empowers that identity through his Holy Spirit which is placed within you so that you can worship and approach him just as Jesus did. The invitation has been offered; will you accept?

Access Not Denied

The customs official looked at me one last time and simply asked me, "What happened to your passport?" I went into full detail of the drama that had surrounded the situation and begged for his mercy. He sat back, thought for a moment, and hesitantly stamped the passport the best he could and with disgust on his voice told me to be on my way.

What a relief! My heart could rest. My identity was confirmed. I boarded the plane and arrived safely in the United States. This illustration reflects much of our relationship with God...except one small part. With God, we don't gain acceptance based upon *our* identity, but upon *his* identity that he gave to us in Christ. He has given us our identity which means we have full access to worship, not based upon who we are, but who he is in us. Without this revelation, worship can never be cultivated. With it, true worship can never be lost.

Application

There is a good chance that some of these thoughts are new and fresh for you. I challenge you to write down some of the traits that you would say characterize your personality. After your list is compiled, go through each trait and ask God if this is who he created you to be. Some will be spot on, and some will seem a million miles from what Jesus displayed.

When you find those traits, simply ask, "God, would you please change this trait I see in myself? I realize that I can't change it in my own strength. I am completely relying upon you to activate your identity in me." As you are praying through these issues, I encourage you to ask close friends to

Milepost 2: The Anchor of Identity

comment on your behaviors and encourage you when they see a change.

Finally, memorize some of the verses used in this chapter and search through Scripture to find references to your new identity. These are helpful when Satan tries to reinforce your false self or when you fall back into operating in your outward man rather than the new inward man. I believe you will be amazed at the results in your life and your worship. It might even feel like a re-birth, an awakening of childlike awe...but that topic belongs in our next chapter.

Chapter 9

Mile Post 3: Childhood Fantasies

There is something to be said for the strong imagination within the heart of a child. It is held in their essence and evidenced in all they think, feel, see, and say. You have seen it...a child can take a simple branch or rock out of the yard, and suddenly they are transported into a magical land I like to call "What if?"

C.S. Lewis knew this magical land well when he wrote the Chronicles of Narnia. To this day I can't watch one of these movies or read one of these books without being brought to tears. Because it speaks to the heart of a child. This leads us to our next milepost in the journey toward an *altared* culture of worship: childlike faith.

One particular story that amazes me is when Lucy catches a glimpse of Aslan the Lion (who symbolizes Christ) in the forest. Her brothers and sisters believe she has been deceived by her own imagination, but she insists that what she has seen is true. Despite the opposition, she resolves to go search for her beloved Aslan while the others are sleeping. Here, read it for yourself.

> "She went fearlessly in among them, dancing herself as she leaped this way and that to avoid being run into by these huge partners [the dancing trees]. But she was only half interested in them. She wanted to get beyond them to something else; it was from beyond them that the dear voice had called.

Milepost 3: Childhood Fantasies

She soon got through them (half wondering whether she had been using her arms to push branches aside, or to take hands in a Great Chain with big dancers who stooped to reach her) for they were really a ring of trees around a central open place.

She stepped out from among their shifting confusion of lovely lights and shadows. A circle of grass, smooth as a lawn, met her eyes, with dark trees dancing all around it. And then – oh joy! For he was there: the huge Lion, shining white in the moonlight, with his huge black shadow underneath him. But for the movement of his tail he might have been a stone lion or not.

She rushed to him. She felt her heart would burst if she lost a moment. And the next thing she knew was that she was kissing him. And putting her arms as far round his neck as she could and burying her face in the beautiful rich silkiness of his mane. "Aslan, Aslan. Dear Aslan." Sobbed Lucy. "At last."

The great beast rolled over on his side so that Lucy fell, half sitting and half lying between his front paws. He bent forward and just touched her nose with his tongue. His warm breath came all round her. She gazed up into the large wise face. "Welcome, child," he said."[xx]

This story is obviously a fairy tale, but for some reason our minds drift easily into this distant world as we paint the picture in our mind. Did you find yourself beginning to imagine this scene from Narnia—to envision the colors and the movement—as you read through this brief excerpt? Why is that? What is in us that makes us re-create the scene? I would suggest that it is God himself.

The God of all creation is seen in everything around us, and amazingly he is seen within us as well. Every human is created in his image, the image of God (see Genesis 1:27). Take just a moment to look at the full spectrum of colors that surround you. His creativity is seen in animals, plants, stars, galaxies, and even the smallest of atoms. With the variety and creativity evidenced in the creation, we are compelled to believe that God has a massive imagination.

Mind of Christ

If in fact God does have a large imagination, there is a strong correlation we can draw from this truth. Keep in mind what we have alluded to earlier: We now have a new identity. Our new identity is established in us when we receive the Holy Spirit, and Paul reminds us that, "We have the mind of Christ" (1 Corinthians 2:16b). This is important because Christ is the one through whom the world was created.

"He is the image of the invisible God, the firstborn of all creation. For by him all things were created, in heaven and on earth, visible and invisible, whether thrones or dominions or rulers or authorities – all things were created through him and for him" (Colossians 1:15-16). We can conclude that since Christ has a massive imagination (which is seen in the creation that was made through him) we too have such an imagination because we were created in God's image and have the mind of Christ.

Why is this correlation significant? Look again at the heart of a child.

A child's heart can be described in a variety of ways because it encompasses so many dimensions–sincerity, faith, wonder, amazement, innocence, creativity, and most importantly imagination. A child is always asking "What if...?

Milepost 3: Childhood Fantasies

What if it could really be true?" Do you think it is by accident that we are called the sons and daughters of God (see Romans 8:15-17, 1 John 4:4)? The answer is a resounding "No!"

I believe we are called the children of God because he desires for us to approach him with the sincerity, faith, wonder, amazement, innocence, creativity, and imagination of a child. Hebrews 11:6 says, "Without faith it is impossible to please him (God) for whoever would draw near to God must believe that he exists and that he rewards those who seek him." Without this childlike approach, rooted in faith, it is impossible to cultivate an intimate relationship with God.

Jesus' Father

Notice that Jesus was constantly referring to what his Father was doing. Jesus references his Father over 283 times throughout the New Testament. Have you recently heard a child speak of their Father? They often come up with outlandish feats in which their father is the victorious hero. Compared to all other fathers, theirs is the best! Their father's accomplishments prevail over all others.

Now, of course we know these stories aren't always true, but in the child's mind their father is the greatest source of strength, security, and comfort they know. It is easy for a child to be led in their imaginations to an exotic list of superlatives. They experience these imaginations vividly because they depend upon their father completely. Children's strong sense of faith leads them to expectations without limitation.

And Jesus was similar in many ways. Like any child, he had faith that his Father could do anything and everything...and in his case, it was actually true! Many argue that Jesus' faith was more complete than ours because of who he was, but remember that *we* are now co-heirs with Jesus, and his Spirit lives within *us* (see 1 Corinthians 8:9). If his Spirit is living inside us, then that same faith has been birthed in us! Our faith in the Father is increasing because of his transforming work within our lives (see 2 Corinthians 3:18).

It is amazing when you think of the supernatural work that is going on inside of you. What if we could approach God like Jesus did? What if we had full assurance in his provision for every need in our lives? I believe that one of the keys to Jesus' intimacy with his Father was his childlike approach. Along with that was his acknowledgement of the rights that came with his son-ship. Once again Jesus himself is demonstrating a key component of a culture of worship: childlikeness.

Let the Children Come to Me

One of the themes in Jesus' teachings is his love for children. Luke 18: 15-17 states, "Now they were bringing even infants to him that he might touch them. And when the disciples saw it, they rebuked them. But Jesus called them to him, saying, 'Let the children come to me, and do not hinder them, for to such belongs the kingdom of God. Truly, I say to you, whoever does not receive the kingdom of God like a child shall not enter it.'"

Why would Jesus say such a thing? What can a child offer, and how can a child benefit the kingdom of God? Children bring what I stated earlier: sincerity, faith, wonder, amazement, innocence, creativity, and (most importantly) imagination. They benefit the kingdom because they demonstrate the ideal heart of a worshiper. Jesus emphasized this relationship between children and the kingdom of God because you can't have one without the other. The heart of a child exudes worship.

It is not coincidence that Jesus was called the "Son of God." Jesus allowed children to come close to him because he lived out that closeness with his Father in the same manner. Jesus knew that when he approached his Father like a child, he was a worshiping him. He also had full assurance that his

Milepost 3: Childhood Fantasies

Father could and would answer his heart's desire when he approached the Father from that posture...because God loves the heart of a child.

He taught on this subject with this illustration... "Which one of you, if his son asks him for bread, will give him a stone? Or if he asks for a fish, will give him a serpent? If you then, who are evil, know how to give good gifts to your children, how much more will your Father who is in heaven give good things to those who ask him?" (Matthew 7:9-11).

What if the reason we don't have is because we don't ask? *What if* we don't experience God the way we desire because this childlike amazement has unconsciously disappeared? Jesus is hitting on something here that is worthy of our attention. We must be aware of and operate in our new identity as a son or daughter of God.

Have you begun to claim your new identity in Christ like we discussed in the last chapter? If not, you have missed the reality that your Father wants to bless you through the gift of his Holy Spirit (see Luke 11:13) as a seal that you are his child (see Ephesians 1:13-14). When these basic truths are misunderstood, people spend their lives trying to earn the favor of God. Instead of faith increasing because of the relationship, distance and doubt envelop the person, inevitably leaving them disengaged and believing themselves to be an orphan.

Doubts of A Child

It is not natural for a child to doubt, but it happens often enough during adolescence. What starts out as a faint whisper of uncertainty as a teenager gives birth to full-blown doubt, distrust, and self-reliance as an adult. We often reason God away with our intellect. We want to trust in things that makes sense and add up—all the while, forgetting that God does not operate within our constraints of time and knowledge.

Instead of childlike wonder and amazement, we become entangled with the trivial, material, and fleeting things of the world. We exchange the faith that our Father can do anything we could ever think or imagine (see Ephesians 3:20) for the innocuous lie that "God can't be trusted." When we fall for this age-old trick (see Genesis 3:1-5), we abandon our rights as sons and daughters...which leads to mistrust, blindness, and deafness to the things of God. Our calloused doubt-ridden outward man imprisons the heart of a child that lives within our inward being, placed there by God himself.

Why is this so devastating? Because it keeps us from experiencing the joy, the blessing, the confidence, and the hope that can only be received by a child. This deceptive whisper comes in a variety of ways, but the consistent result is disengagement and forfeiture of our rights as sons and daughters of God.

Is Aslan Really Here?

Although Lucy found the mysterious Aslan by listening for his voice and searching the dark forest, her brothers Peter and Edmond and her sister Susan doubted the story entirely and dismissed it as fantasy. C.S Lewis continues the tale,

> "When the whole party was finally awake, Lucy had to tell her story for the fourth time. The blank silence which followed it was as discouraging as anything could be.
>
> "I can't see anything," said Peter after he had stared his eyes sore. "Can you, Susan?"
>
> "No, of course I can't," snapped Susan. "Because there isn't anything to see. She's been dreaming."[xxi]

Milepost 3: Childhood Fantasies

Later on in the story, Lucy is leading her siblings through the forest as she follows the lead of Aslan. Lewis writes,

> "The others had only Lucy's direction to guide them, for Aslan was not only invisible to them but silent as well. His big cat-like paws made no noise on the grass."[xxii]

Finally, they get to their destination, and everybody is ecstatic that Aslan has been found, not knowing that he was with them all along the journey, protecting them from harm. They are faced with their own disbelief and distrust in Aslan. Susan's doubt is realized as she meets the large lion.

> "Then after an awful pause, the deep voice said, "Susan." Susan made no answer but the others thought she was crying. "You have listened to fears, child," said Aslan. "Come, let me breathe on you. Forget them. Are you brave again?" "A little, Aslan," said Susan."[xxiii]

Let's dig into some of the truths that Lewis is hitting in this story. All children experience fear, but the child who correctly understands their relationship to the father runs *to* God in the midst of uncertain circumstance. As Lucy did. On the other hand, Susan represents the child who doubts the relationship that was rightfully hers because of a spirit of fear...doubt which led her to lose sight of Aslan.

John Bevere states, "Those who are afraid, draw back from him, but those who fear him draw toward him."[xxiv] As followers of Christ, we have all experienced this disabling fear that leads us to lose sight of God and grow deaf to his voice. This is rooted in our own lack of knowledge of the entitlement of sons and daughters. Instead of a childlike freedom with God that asks, "What if?" we settle for disengaged anxiety which asks, "Are you really here?" Can you see the fundamental difference in the two? Faith is the very essence of the first and the very opposite of the second.

Childlike Culture of Worship

I hope you have seen that an *altared* culture of worship must contain this childlike excitement, expectancy, and faith. A culture that is based upon this connective relationship with God is living and vibrant. Its members are always dreaming big dreams, setting big goals, and believing not that God *might* do the impossible, but *will* do the impossible in their culture and generation.

I believe God is calling us to ask, "What if?" again. *What if* my friend got saved? *What if* that person was really healed? *What if* we really could connect and worship with God like Jesus? *What if* a revival swept through a whole city, state, or nation? Remember Jesus' words, "Ask, and it will be given to you; seek, and you will find; knock, and it will be opened to you. For everyone who asks receives, and the one who seeks finds, and to the one who knocks it will be opened" (Matthew 7:7-8). Don't you think we are entitled to some pretty awesome things as children of God? For far too long doubt has reigned over the Church, and it is time for us to embrace the childlike faith that is rightfully ours as God's children.

When we doubt his provision and are unsure of our relational intimacy as children, it is almost impossible to come before God with a faith that pleases him (see Hebrews 11:6). The reason that we don't experience him more in our lives is because of our skewed mindset, not a lack of God's goodness. Throughout scripture God constantly reminds us of his love for his children.

We see this love portrayed through Paul, "For I am sure that neither death nor life, nor angels nor rulers, nor things present nor things to come, nor powers, nor height nor depth, nor anything else in all creation, will be able to separate us from the love of God in Christ Jesus our Lord" (Romans 8:37-

Milepost 3: Childhood Fantasies

39). Blindness to this love leads to doubt, disengagement, and a false identity, but when you understand and relate to God as his child, your life will be marked by extreme confidence, acceptance, and expectation.

If I had to pick between those two descriptions, I would go with the second option, wouldn't you? Of course, we all would because that is how Jesus approached his Father. His Spirit within us cries out from the deepest parts of our inward man for a childlike approach to our Father.

When is the last time you asked God, "What if?" with expectancy and confidence that his presence would blow your mind? We spend most of our lives trying to put away our childhood imagination, but Jesus is reminding us that until we approach him like a child, we'll never get it. You will never know how to truly worship and never see the supernatural that is ours to experience until we worship like a child.

Application

I hope as you read through this chapter that you were reminded of and encouraged by the love of God that is available to his children. If you have struggled with this relationship over the years, don't worry; you are not alone. Many adults try to approach everything with reason and logic, even their relationship with God. I invite you to wonder again. Ask, "What if God could do _____?"

Well, the good news is that he can do anything. Here is a hint, though: He loves his kingdom and anything that is going to advance his good news throughout the world. He is very passionate about you, as any Father would be over his son or daughter.

Sift through your own heart and ask yourself what lies you have erroneously believed about your relationship to your Father. It could be that you thought he was demanding, disloyal, abusive, absent, or displeased with you because that is the way your earthy father related to you. Ask God, not to erase those memories, but to reveal to you the new Father-son or Father-daughter relationship he is establishing in your life.

Accept his love. Don't reject it because of your own pride, distrust, or bitterness. Invite God into those places and emotions; you'll be amazed at the healing that comes from understanding your proper relationship with God. Next, read through Luke 15:11-32, the story of the prodigal son. Put yourself in the place of the younger son and meditate on God's response to you because of who you are and not because of what you have done.

Finally, dream like a child! Look at the world through eyes of expectation and ask "What if?" Maybe, just maybe, you will be like Lucy and be able to see and hear God with clarity when others have grown deaf, dumb, and blind. An essential component of worship is to approach God like a child.

Chapter 10

Milepost 4: Choose What Is Best

I was starting to worry.

It had happened on two different occasions, but I still didn't know why. The first time I was on my way to school, and the second time I was just sitting at the race track with my father. I remember asking my dad if it was normal for a person's heart to beat out of rhythm and he told me, "You are young, don't worry about it." Well, on this particular night I couldn't help but worry about it.

My heart seemed to stop and start and sputter over and over again. It completely took my breath away, and I wondered if I was having a heart attack. Finally, I decided it was time to go to the hospital. When I got there, I was rushed back like any heart patient would be. They strapped a big machine to all parts of my body and started taking blood. I had no idea what was going on, and I was scared.

After a few hours the doctor came back and asked me some questions. "Could you please describe your schedule to me?" and "Do you drink a lot of caffeine?" I explained to him that I was a full-time student, worked two part-time jobs with little time for rest, and that yes, I did drink sodas but not what I thought was an excessive amount.

After listening to my responses, he told me that my EKG was fine. I was simply suffering from stress in my life. I was working too hard and drinking too much caffeine to keep me going. He suggested that I take a break and lay off the soft drinks for a few weeks. Relieved, I took his advice and set out to find relaxation. This is where the story gets good.

The Path to a New Culture

Man Overboard

At the time I was working as a church intern and decided to take a break from Sunday morning. I thought, nothing could be more relaxing than taking my boat out on the lake Sunday morning, alone with God and my Bible. When I got there, it was just as I expected, calm and beautiful. I launched my boat and found a secluded cove where I could be alone.

Everything was going great until I heard my motor making a strange noise. Turning around to check it out, I was stunned to find that my motor was actually on fire! And when I saw that the motor was still connected to the gas tank, I panicked. I grabbed my keys and wallet and was poised to dive overboard, thinking she was going to blow.

But in a last minute shot of heroism, I ventured back through the flames to disconnect the gas. I reached for the gas line, pulled hard, and the line broke. Surprisingly, my hand was not burned, so I started using the most available resource at hand: water. I splashed as much as I could over the engine with the intent of extinguishing the flames. After much stress and sweat, the fire was contained.

I eased down into my seat, my heart about to beat out of my chest. Was this the good life of rest and relaxation that God intended? After a few hours I finally flagged down another boat to tow me back. And as I reflected on the day, being pulled behind another boat toward the marina, I had to admit that I didn't know the first thing about resting.

Running Ragged

The fourth milepost along our journey is rest. When average Americans think about rest, they are usually engulfed by thoughts of confusion and frustration. We own a desire, deeply rooted within our being, that longs for rest...but the culture we live in does not value it as an essential component of life. Americans work incessantly, chasing the elusive dream

Milepost 4: Choose What Is Best

of retirement, often only to find it is not all we dreamed. We have lost something along the way, and that something is the ability to rest.

Our culture is built of heart attacks, stress, tension, and the bottom line. Our relationships, our health, and our very lives are burned to smoke and ashes upon the altar of success. We willingly gamble our integrity and character for the chance at obtaining our self-absorbed goals. Our longing for material possessions, a prominent position, and a name for ourselves which is engrained into our soul by our very culture.

In this culture, rest is reserved for the aged. The ones who obtain their ambitions earn the reward of rest...and usually don't know what to do with it. For everyone else, rest remains the elusive carrot we run after. Like a rabbit, we chase the prize, only to be left disappointed and embarrassed at having fallen for the same old trick again. In other words, the world's formula is work now; rest later. And as usual, God's method for his children is the opposite: rest first and work later.

God's Method

God's vision for rest can be broken into two distinct components: spiritual and physical. The spiritual component of rest is focused upon our identity and relationship with Christ. Physical rest, on the other hand, is commanded by God for our own health...and the powerful acknowledgement of his deliverance in our lives. What is God delivering us from? The slavery of works.

Without God's intervention we are all left enslaved to our flesh and to the wisdom of this world (see 1 Corinthians 3:19-20). God's theme throughout the history of humanity is freedom. It's displayed in the great exodus from Egyptian oppression all the way to Jesus' teaching and ultimate sacrifice. Galatians 5:1 states, "For freedom Christ set us free." If that is the case, let's figure out how rest applies to our freedom.

Physical Rest

The relationship between worship and physical rest is seen in the exodus of God's people from Egyptian oppression. God presented his purpose for setting the captives free when he told Moses, "And you shall say to him [pharaoh], 'The Lord, the God of the Hebrews, sent me to you, saying, "Let my people go, that they may worship me in the wilderness"'" (Exodus 7:16).

The Israelites had settled in the region of Goshen in Eqypt due to Joseph's prominence but had subsequently been forced into slavery. After the death of pharaoh a new successor to the throne had become leery of the magnitude of the Israelite people. He believed that if war broke out, the Israelites would join Egypt's enemies and fight against them. Out of his fear he decided to place them under the oppression of slavery. They were forced to make bricks to build the mighty edifices that characterized the Egyptian empire (see Exodus 1:11-14).

Under the grueling work they were crying out for rest and deliverance from God. In response he spoke to Moses and told him, "I have surely seen the affliction of my people who are in Egypt and have heard their cry because of their taskmasters. I know their sufferings, and I have come down to deliver them out of the hand of the Egyptians and to bring them up out of the land to a good and broad land, a land flowing with milk and honey" (Exodus 3:7-8).

With deliverance and rest being God's intent let's re-examine the words we just previously read in that light, "Let my people go, that they may worship me in the wilderness" (Exodus 7:16). The people of God were freed and invited to rest from their work in order to worship God.

Early in the story we see the correlation of rest, or deliverance from slavery and oppression, to the worship of God. After the Israelites received their freedom, God again reminded them that they were supposed to rest for the purpose of remembrance. "Above all you shall keep my

Milepost 4: Choose What Is Best

Sabbaths, for this is a sign between me and you throughout your generations, that you may know that I the Lord, sanctify you" (Exodus 31:12). They were to remember that God was their provision; he brought them out of slavery and toil to a place where they could experience rest.

Fast-forward to the New Testament, and let's look at Jesus' instruction on physical rest and worship. Luke 10:38-42 says,

> "Now as they went on their way, Jesus entered a village. And a woman named Martha welcomed him into her house. And she had a sister called Mary, who sat at the Lord's feet and listened to his teaching. But Martha was distracted with much serving. And she went up to him and said, "Lord, do you not care that my sister has left me to serve alone? Tell her then to help me." But the Lord answered her, "Martha, Martha, you are anxious and troubled about many things, but one thing is necessary. Mary has chosen the good portion, which will not be taken from her."

In this story we see two responses to Jesus. Martha was consumed with meeting the physical needs of her Savior. This is not to be demeaned. I believe she was passionate in her love for Jesus; she just allowed her love to be expressed through her work as the way to please him...which ironically distanced her from the one she desired to please. Many of us make the same mistake. We get caught up in the physical, outward acts that display love for God. The intention is pure but at times misdirected. We often feel, "Who has time to rest?"

Please notice that in this story Jesus did not stop Martha. He continued to teach and speak the words of life. Jesus did not stop Martha from her work because, just like us, she was too preoccupied and busy to listen. Isn't this far too often true in our own lives?

Author Joanna Weaver writes, "Mary, on the other hand, understands what is necessary, to physically rest at the feet of Jesus. It is only in this place that one can hear. Jesus even comments that it is necessary. 'Necessary for what?' It is necessary for life and worship, for without it, life is not what God intended. Mary understood the difference between worship and work."[xxv] Worship is not so much about doing, but resting.

Weaver continues, "This is a story of two different responses to one singular occasion. In it, we should find not our personality type, but the kind of heart Christ longs for us to have. A heart centered on him alone."[xxvi] God is inviting us to rest from our physical endeavors to sit at his feet and worship. He simply says, "Choose what is best."

Spiritual Rest

As I stated earlier, spiritual rest focuses on our identity and relationship with God. It is important to note that this component is the most misunderstood of the two because of the culture in which we live. As Christians we often allow the values of our culture to seep into our relationship with God, which contaminates the purity of that relationship. This happens because the principles of our culture are often in direct opposition to God. Therefore, we are prone to attempt to earn God's favor in the same way that we work and labor for our own natural success.

This misconception is due to an incorrect view of God…and our own identity. Rest assured, this is not a new problem. It has plagued God's people from the beginning of our existence.

We first see the idea of rest after God created the world. "Thus the heavens and the earth were finished, and all the host of them. And on the seventh day God finished his work

Milepost 4: Choose What Is Best

that he had done, and he rested on the seventh day from all his work that he had done. So God blessed the seventh day and made it holy, because on it God rested from all his work that he had done in creation" (Genesis 2:1-3).

Notice that this day of rest is the first thing in all of God's creation that he calls "holy." A great deal of importance is symbolized by this act. God works first and then rests after his work in completed. Mankind's life, on the other hand, begins on this sacred and holy day of rest. Watchman Nee states,

> "Adam, we are told, was created on the sixth day. Clearly, then, he had no part in those first six days of work, for he came into being only at their end. God's seventh day was, in fact, Adam's first. Whereas God worked six days and then enjoyed the Sabbath rest, Adam began his life with the Sabbath; for God works before he rests, while man must first enter into God's rest, and then alone can he work."[xxvii]

Within this example we can hear a faint whisper of the gospel resonating. We were created to live in such a way that God is our sole solution to the work of salvation. We can rest from that work because of the complete work of Christ on our behalf (see Colossians 1:19-20). The innate striving to labor and earn now must die that we may experience the intimacy of God's gift. Our tendency to labor was not God's intention; however, this temptation is common to all of us because of sin.

After Adam and Eve sinned, God claimed, "Cursed is the ground because of you; in pain you shall eat of it all the days of your life; thorns and thistles it shall bring forth, for you; and you shall eat the plants of the field. By the sweat of your face you shall eat bread" (Gen.3:17b-19a). Notice that labor replaces rest. Before their sin Adam and Eve ate freely from trees and plants they did not grow. God was their sole provision. After their sin, they now had to labor with sweat, blood, and tears for the same food that previously they so easily obtained. Thus, our work and striving began.

As you read those words, you may think that I am contradicting Scripture. After all, Genesis 2:15 clearly states, "The Lord God took the man and put him in the Garden of Eden to work it and keep it." If you look at this verse at face value, it appears that God always intended man to work. On the other hand if you look at the original Hebrew language, there is a strong suggestion that instead of working in and keeping the garden, God had something far greater in mind.

Dr. John Sailhamer states, "A more suitable translation of the Hebrew would be 'to worship and to obey.' Man is put in the garden to worship God and to obey him. Man's life in the garden was to be characterized by worship and obedience; he was a priest, not merely a worker and keeper of the garden." (For further explanation refer to the endnote.)[xxviii]

If we were indeed created to worship and obey, then that is at the core of our being. However, due to the fall of Adam and the curse of sin, all of mankind has been led to the direct opposite from that day forward. Ever since, mankind has struggled with the practice of rest. A labor mindset became the craving of the culture of the world by default, and man still lives under its bondage. But through the sacrifice of Jesus, we now have the ability to rest again in our relationship with God.

The author of Hebrews illustrates this rest when he tells the story of the Israelite people.

> "Therefore, as the Holy Spirit says, "Today, if you hear his voice, do not harden your hearts as in the rebellion, on the day of testing in the wilderness, where your fathers put me to the test and saw my works for the forty years. Therefore I was provoked with that generation, and said, 'They always go astray in their heart; they have not known my ways.' As

Milepost 4: Choose What Is Best

I swore in my wrath, 'They shall not enter my rest.'" (Hebrews 3:7-11)

He continues,

"For who were those who heard and yet rebelled? Was it not all those who left Egypt led by Moses? And with whom was he provoked forty years? Was it not with those who sinned, whose bodies fell in the wilderness? And to whom did he swear they would not enter his rest, but to those who were disobedient? So we see that they were unable to enter because of unbelief." (Hebrews 3:16-19)

God's invitation to his people has always been to enter his rest. After the first failed attempt, the Israelites were again invited by God to enter Canaan, the symbol of their rest, after the previous unbelieving generation had died. They were given the opportunity to live in a land where they would eat from vineyards they didn't plant and drink from wells they did not dig (see Deuteronomy 8:4-10). This sounds a lot like the way the story began, doesn't it?

Again, God wanted them to see that he was their sole provision. He wanted to bring his people back to the garden. He was in the process of restoring this most precious relationship, but they forfeited intimacy by their unbelief. They chose to place their worship and trust in themselves rather than in him. And people are making the same mistake today. Worship is about trust and obedience and making God our source.

The writer of Hebrews continues, "'Today if you hear his voice, do not harden your hearts.' There remains a Sabbath rest for the people of God, for whoever has entered God's rest has also rested from his works as God did from his. Let us therefore strive to enter that rest, so that no one may fall by the same sort of disobedience" (Hebrews 4:9-11). There are two main points from this passage. First, we are prone to disobedience, and second, we must strive to enter the spiritual rest that God provides through Christ.

I believe that God allows us to operate within a culture of labor so we will be hungry for the invitation to rest. Only as the juxtaposition of these two cultures comes to light can we understand and choose true worship. We must acknowledge that our labor to earn is empty and fruitless in our relationship with God.

Ephesians 2:8 states, "For by grace you have been saved through faith. And this is not your own doing; it is the gift of God, not a result of works, so that no one may boast." Do you see the beauty of this gift? We no longer have to labor in a desperate attempt to earn God's favor. It is freely ours because of the sacrifice of Christ. It's his provision, and our new identity as God's child allows us to rest from our work (John 1:12). Just as God invited the Israelites to enter the rest of the Promised Land, he is now inviting us to rest in Christ.

Listen to Jesus' words when he said, "Take my yoke upon you, and learn from me, for I am gentle and lowly in heart, and you will find rest for your souls. For my yoke is easy, and my burden is light" (Matthew 11:29-30). We have God's approval once and for all, which frees us from labor and the yoke of slavery.

The Struggle

Although most of us understand rest as a physical concept, we often miss its significance in our relationship with Christ. We still work to rid ourselves of sin. In other words, we are still striving to be holy, still laboring for righteousness in our lives. And because of that, many Christians are plagued with guilt and condemnation because they can't achieve it.

Milepost 4: Choose What Is Best

They know that God requires it (see 1 Peter 1:16), but they feel their striving is in vain.

What if God never meant for us to *achieve* holiness? You might be saying to yourself, "Now, wait just a minute; aren't we supposed to strive for holiness?" After all, God has not called us to impurity, but to holiness (see 1 Thessalonians 4:7). Many Christians live in enormous inner tension because they don't understand their identity and what God's Holy Spirit has done in them. They still are working as hard as they can to be moral and keep the rules, when in reality, that's not why God established rules in the first place.

The law was set before us to help us realize that we *can't* keep God's commands, that we need a Savior (see Romans 7:4-6). I am convinced that far too many of us are still laboring in the fields, striving to please their Father, when the provision and the rest of God are available for the taking (see Luke 15:25-32).

Spiritual Worship

Let's look at a familiar passage on worship. Romans 12:1 says, "I appeal to you therefore, brothers, by the mercies of God, to present your bodies as a living sacrifice, holy and acceptable to God, which is your spiritual worship." The living sacrifice, which is our lives, is not holy and acceptable based upon what we as individuals have done. We are holy and acceptable because of the new identity that was birthed in us when the Holy Spirit took up residence within us (see 1 Corinthians 3:17 & 1 Peter 2:9-10).

If we desire to be delivered from sin, the appropriate response is not to do a particular task to earn God's favor, but to rest in our new identity that he has already established. God is revealing to us through his word that he has already completed the work. Not only are we now holy and acceptable to him because God sees us through Jesus' sacrifice, but God is continually transforming us into his image (see 2 Corinthians

3:18). Until we understand this, we will never cease from doing works to earn God's approval.

God, because of his love, will patiently allow us to labor on...until we recognize that he is the one that must bring about this change in our lives. Nee comments, "God is waiting for your store of strength to be utterly exhausted before he can deliver you. Once you have ceased to struggle, he will do everything. God is waiting for you to despair."[xxix] Only at this moment can rest be experienced in the life of a worshiper.

This surrender is the sacrifice that God calls "spiritual worship." When submission takes place in our lives, everything we do becomes worship. Mark Buchanan comments,

> "The opposite of a slave is not a free man. It's a worshiper. The one who is most free is the one who turns the work of his hands into sacrament, into offering. All he makes, all he does are gifts from God, through God, and to God. Virtually any job no matter how grueling or tedious – any job that is not criminal or sinful – can be a gift from God, through God, and to God. The work of our hands, by the alchemy of our devotion, becomes the worship of our hearts."[xxx]

Spiritual worship is pleasing to God (see John 4:24), but it can only be achieved through a spirit of rest in our inward man. When God brings an individual to a place of brokenness and despair in their own abilities to achieve holiness, he opens their eyes not only to his provision in their life but also to his acceptance of them.

When one receives approval from a superior, it brings an attitude of great confidence and thankfulness. They desire no longer to please their Father through working or keeping rules, but to bless him with the offering of their life. Everything that is done in this attitude constitutes worship.

A Culture of Rest

So, how does this idea of rest relate to an *altared* culture of worship? I believe rest is found at the very center of what God is calling us to create. When rest is not present, worry, anxiety, and tension plague the church and the individual. Faith in God is diminished when self-reliance permeates and contaminates the atmosphere. An individual can't effectively come to God in prayer while simultaneously believing that anything that is going to happen is up to them.

Focusing on failures and striving after unattainable goals disables the Christian from singing songs of praise. This leads to discouragement and disengagement. Likewise, there can be no peace or joy in the life burdened with the relentless task of earning God's favor.

For those who are somewhat able to keep the rules and appear holy to others, one of two things is happening: 1) They are in a constant battle due to the hypocritical contradiction between the attitude of their hearts and their outward appearance, or 2) They have a false security in their ability to stay away from major sins.

On the opposite end of the spectrum, there are individuals who are aware of their own inability to be holy, and who give up, deciding to live for themselves. In neither case are people experiencing God's great intent. They understand worship only as an outward act but fail to engage God's invitation to rest in him.

When rest is the attitude of a culture, all the walls and pretenses come down. There is no need to *appear* holy because there is recognition of the holiness of God within us. Those who dwell in this culture experience an authenticity of worship. Worship is not only the internal, intimate relationship between the individual and God, but it also permeates every act, job, and relationship within that culture.

Finally, rest allows us to hear God speaking. Remember Jesus' example in John 5:19-20, "Truly, truly, I say to you, the Son can do nothing of his own accord, but only what he sees the Father doing. For whatever the Father does, that the Son does likewise. For the Father loves the Son and shows him all that he himself is doing." If we are indeed children, which we are, then we are invited to experience God in the same way that Jesus did. After all, scripture states, "The sheep [us] hear his [Jesus'] voice, and he calls his own sheep by name and leads them out. He goes before them, and the sheep follow him for they know his voice" (John 10:3-4).

One main condition to this is that we understand how to rest in God. Mark Buchanan states,

> "God is always speaking. "There is no speech or language where his voice is not heard" (Psalm 19:3). But we're not always listening. We don't make the effort and so fail to go boldly into his throne room to receive what we need: a word that can pierce and cut and heal. If we don't listen, we never enter his rest. Yet if we don't enter his rest, we never listen."[xxxi]

God is inviting us to hear the words of life that proceed out of his mouth. We must stop and rest from the busyness and clutter that encompasses our schedule and consumes our soul. When is the last time you stopped to listen, to really hear the voice of God? It's time to stop striving, working, and performing. Only then will you be able to hear the gentle whisper of your Father (see 1 Kings 19:12). He pleads, "Choose me, choose what is best!"

Milepost 4: Choose What Is Best

Application

I am well aware that all I have shared is in direct opposition to the culture that surrounds us, but I also know that this is where life is found. Most of us who have operated in our world's culture for any length of time have come to the revelation that it isn't working. We are more frustrated than we have ever been because of our lack of personal growth in our relationship with God. Could it be that God has arranged your circumstances to allow you to come to the end of yourself?

I invite you to pause and begin to look at and evaluate all the things in your life that are currently leaving you frustrated and unfulfilled. There is a good chance that you are still operating in the world's culture of busyness and success instead of living in the rest of God. Evaluate how you are approaching God. Are you still trying to earn his favor? Have you learned to spiritually rest?

After you have sifted through the clutter and lies, switch to the physical dimension. There is good chance that most of you have run yourself so ragged that you have forgotten how to live with adequate sleep and refreshment. Where can you begin to set aside time to rest, dream, listen, and play?

When you identify these times, ask your spouse or friends to constantly remind you to rest. As you begin to implement this spiritual and physical rest, you will find life for the first time. Welcome to life God's way!

Chapter 11

Milepost 5: *Altaring* Moments

Everything seemed to be going as planned. I had all my tasks checked off, and I was ready to lead my first real mission trip. As a youth intern, I was given the responsibility of scheduling all the summer excursions of our youth group. And this was no small task: There were buses to rent, events to plan, hotels to reserve, travel maps to print, Bible studies to write, and food to prepare. The list went on and on!

The work was divided between three interns, and I was working with travel, food, and hotels. Before the summer started, I had been working for a month straight, trying to find the best deals and checking availability. I was almost certain that I had everything under control.

When we arrived at the first night's hotel, everything went as planned. We checked in, had just the right number of rooms, and everybody got their sleeping arrangements.

Just as we were getting ready to settle down for the night, my pastor asked me what time the continental breakfast started. "Umm," I stuttered. He asked, "They do have continental breakfast, right? Because we have no food, no place to prepare it, and no place to eat." At that moment I knew that I had made a pretty big blunder. I asked, "What do you want me to do?" He answered, "You are going to have to figure it out; this is your responsibility."

I stood there in the parking lot, baffled that I could have made such a mistake. How could I have forgotten such a huge detail? Everyone else headed off for bed, as it was already well past midnight. *What was even open at this time?* I asked myself, *And where could I find enough food to feed 150 people?*

Milepost 5: *Altaring* Moments

I found a local Wal-Mart and walked the aisles in desperation, just hoping that I could find something to fill their stomachs. As I walked down the cereal aisle, a brilliant idea came to me. Cereal is cheap, and you don't have to heat it up. One box can feed a bunch of people! So, I loaded a shopping cart full.

The only problem with cereal is that we would need milk…and there were no refrigerators in our rooms. Just when it seemed my plans had been thwarted, I remembered that each hotel has an ice machine. I bought about 10 gallons of milk and headed back to the hotel. I told the guys in the room that they were not going to get a shower in the morning because our bathtub was going to be converted into an ice cooler.

After what felt like fifty trips to the ice machine with our little bucket, we filled the entire bath tub with ice and placed the milk inside. The next morning when breakfast was finally complete, I realized the powerful lesson that forgetting details can dramatically alter a desired outcome.

The Plague of Forgetfulness

It is easy for most of us to identify with stories like that because we all have stories of our own; we have all dropped the ball in some form or fashion. And if we are honest, we will admit that "forgetfulness" pervades our culture. We constantly witness someone else's busyness causing them to forget important details. Parents forget to pick up their children, spouses forget their own anniversaries, and employees forget countless meetings.

What is the cause of this plague of forgetfulness? I believe it is rooted in being consumed with our own agenda. This often shows up when we communicate with others. We actually forget the details of conversations because we are only hearing and focusing on our own thoughts, not the other person's.

My concern is that we bring this same forgetfulness into our relationship with Christ. When we do find time in our busy schedules to pray, it is often one-sided. The busyness that engulfs us actually fosters forgetfulness, which leads to disengagement with the One who created us. We frantically say everything that comes to mind, ask God to bless it, and quickly move on with our day. But we forget that prayer is a two-sided relationship and involves just as much listening as speaking. We settle for the one-sided version that lacks the intimacy that our hearts truly desire.

Our prayers become so self-focused, self-absorbed, and mindless that we often forget what we have prayed. This mindless mechanical form of prayer does not even allow us to thank God for his answers… because the petition is so quickly forgotten.

The Path to a New Culture

Throughout this last section of the book we have identified different mileposts that help us mark our journey and help us remember the past steps. The mileposts offer a more in-depth look into the critical components that must be present for this new culture to thrive. The stories that have been told are lessons learned and experiences gathered that I learned along my path to create an *altared* culture of worship.

In this particular chapter I will develop the idea that this newly proposed culture of worship is based upon what I call *altaring* moments. I will show how a lack of remembrance is the major contributing factor to the church's lack of authentic worship in our world today. A forgetting of Jesus' example as well as forgetting God's steadfastness prohibits us from leading others to worship. This forgetfulness is not unique to our culture; it has plagued people groups and individuals for centuries. One culture in particular comes to mind: the Israelites.

Milepost 5: *Altaring* Moments

Remember the Journey

Throughout Israel's journey we see a recurring theme of forgetfulness and a constant directive to remember. God, through his anointed leaders and prophets, instructed the people of Israel to commit to memory his acts of deliverance.

We first see that remembering is important to God when he is preparing the Israelites to enter into the Promised Land for the first time. After years of wandering through the desert, God said, "And you shall *remember* the whole way that the Lord your God has led you these forty years in the wilderness, that he might humble you, testing you to know what was in your heart" (Deuteronomy 8:2).

He goes on to remind them of his provision of clothing, health, and food (see v. 3-10). All along the journey he reminded them, through Moses, that he was the one who heard their cry for mercy and set them free from the yoke of slavery (see Numbers 33:3-4). There was a constant recounting of this freedom story so that no one would forget what God had done. The story and commandments were so important that they were supposed to be constantly taught to children, discussed frequently, and even written upon the very doors and gates of their houses (see Deuteronomy 6:7-9).

As they were entering the land for the second time, God warned them, "Take care lest you *forget* the Lord your God by not keeping his commandments and rules and his statutes, which I command you today" (Deuteronomy 8:11). He went on to say, "And when the Lord your God brings you into the land that he swore to your fathers, to Abraham, to Isaac, and to Jacob, to give you—with great and good cities that you did not build, and houses full of all good things that you did not fill, and cisterns that you did not dig, and vineyards and olive trees that you did not plant—and when you eat and are full, then take care lest you *forget* the Lord, who brought you out of the land of Egypt, out of the house of slavery" (Deuteronomy 6:10-12, italics added for emphasis).

God knows that when a culture of forgetfulness takes root in us, it is the end of the intimate relationship he desires with us. So we can conclude that remembrance allows us to connect with God and is a key component in a worship culture.

Memory Rocks

Scripture carries on the theme of remembrance through the passing of leadership. As we continue in the story, Moses has been informed of his pending death and has begun the process of passing his authority to Joshua (see Deuteronomy 34). Joshua assembled the twelve tribes of the nation and again prepared Israel to enter the Promised Land.

The first seemingly insurmountable obstacle in their path is the Jordan River. God commanded Joshua to take the Ark of the Covenant into the river and then delivered the nation by causing the water of the river to rise up in a heap, which allowed his people to pass on dry ground (see Joshua 3:15-17). Let's pick up the story after they had crossed.

> "When all the nation had finished passing over the Jordan, The Lord said to Joshua, "Take twelve men from the people, from each tribe a man, and command them saying, 'Take twelve stones from here out of the midst of the Jordan, from the very place where the priests' feet stood firmly, and bring them over with you and lay them down in the place where you lodge tonight.'"
>
> "Then Joshua called the twelve men from the people of Israel, whom he had appointed, a man from each tribe. And Joshua said to them, "Pass on before the ark of the Lord your God into the midst of the Jordan, and take up each of you a stone upon his shoulder, according to

Milepost 5: *Altaring* Moments

the number of the tribes of the people of Israel, that this may be a sign among you. *When your children ask in the time to come, 'What do those stones mean to you?'* then you shall tell them that the waters of the Jordan were cut off before the ark of the covenant of the Lord. When it passed over the Jordan, the waters of the Jordan were cut off. So *these stones shall be to the people of Israel a memorial forever.*"

"And the people of Israel did just as Joshua commanded and took up twelve stones out of the midst of the Jordan, according to the number of the tribes of the people of Israel, just as the Lord told Joshua. And they carried them over with them to the place where they lodged and laid them down there. And Joshua set up twelve stones in the midst of the Jordan, in the place where the feet of the priests bearing the Ark of the Covenant had stood; and *they are there to this day"* (Joshua 4:1-9, italics added for emphasis).

As we sift through this story, I'd like to highlight three statements that I believe define the proposed culture and extract their meaning. 1) *When your children ask in the time to come, "What do those stones mean to you?"* Notice that the memorial stones had the purpose, not only to remind the current generation of God's provision, but also to instruct future generations of the events that transpired on that day. 2) *These stones shall be to the people of Israel a memorial forever.* God used a substance that was not easily destroyed or moved. A rock is seemingly insignificant. It has little to no value, but it symbolizes a mighty act and is used to remind God's people to commit his provision to memory. 3) *They are there to this day.* When this story was written in Scripture, the author reminds us that the stones are still there, beckoning us to acknowledge the acts of God, serving as a reminder of what he has done.

Israel's Mistake...and Ours

Joshua seemed to have eradicated the problem of forgetfulness as he faithfully followed all that the Lord commanded. However, things are not always what they seem on the surface. By the end of Joshua's life, Israel had already forgotten the Lord's provision. Judges 2:12b-13 says, "They went after other gods, from among the gods of the peoples who were around them, and bowed down to them. They abandoned the Lord and served the Baals and the Ashtaroth."

How could this happen? How could people see miracles of water standing up in a pile and enemies defeated every turn and still forget God? I believe it is because they did not commit to memory the acts of God. They did not understand that the memorial rocks would preserve and protect their relationship with God. Without memory of the steps, the journey is forgotten.

It is easy to look critically at history and say to ourselves, "If I was there, I wouldn't have made that mistake," but as we have all heard it said, *Hindsight is 20/20.* We are all prone to make the same mistake in our generation. We have all failed to remember at some point the steps that God has taken us through to get us to where we stand today.

When we forget the processes and lessons learned along the journey, we are often led down the same path again! God is determined for us to learn the lessons that ultimately bring us into intimacy with God. This forgetfulness also leaves us susceptible to buy the lie of Satan that God is not good.

We all know there are times in our life when it is hard to see God's goodness. At these moments we are called to remember the faithfulness and steadfastness of God throughout the steps of our journey (see Psalm 26:3). The engulfing cloud of our circumstances often obscures our

Milepost 5: *Altaring* Moments

ability to see God's purpose in the present trial. But if we recall God's faithfulness, we will not abandon the hope and faith that we have in Christ (see Colossians 1:21-23). When we do forget, we forfeit our victory and the intimacy that are ours for the taking.

Forgetfulness Robs Us of Faith

Shortly after Jesus had fed five thousand people with five loaves of bread, and then fed another four thousand people with five loaves of bread, he and his disciples were traveling by boat to another city (see Mark 8:1-10,14). At some point, they realized that they had forgotten to bring bread. Panicked, they been to discuss what they would do for their next meal (see Mark 8:16).

Jesus said to them, "Why are you discussing the fact that you have no bread? Do you not perceive or understand? Are your hearts hardened? Having eyes do you not see, and having ears do you not hear? And do you not remember? When I broke the five loaves for five thousand...?" (Mark 8:17-19) The disciples made the mistake that we identified earlier: They did not realize the supernatural moment they were experiencing.

They failed to stop, worship, and make an altar of remembrance in their mind. They had forgotten the details. This disabled them from having faith that he could feed twelve...when they had previously seen him feed well over 9,000 people! Jesus is inviting us to remember his provision; this act of worship will enable us to have greater faith in what the future holds.

Altaring Moments

I would like to propose a new, fresh concept that helps us to connect with God in these moments of confusion. I like to call them *altaring* moments. Yes, I know it is normally spelled altering, but I am referencing the Old Testament "*altar*."

The Path to a New Culture

I know many of you are saying to yourselves, "We live under a new covenant, and we are no longer under the law." I am aware of that fact and am actually rather excited that I don't have to kill animals all the time and wave their fat in the air. I am, however, interested in taking what the *altar* symbolized and applying it to our current context and culture.

If you investigate the history of the Israelite people, you will see altars are scattered throughout their story. Noah built an altar to the Lord after exiting the ark (see Genesis 8:20), Jacob was instructed to offer his son Isaac on an altar (see Genesis 22), Moses built an altar after receiving water from the rock (see Exodus 17:15) and receiving the Ten Commandments (see Exodus 20:25), and Joshua constructed an altar after receiving a new covenant at Mount Ebal (see Joshua 8:30).

David built an altar to the Lord when bringing the Ark of the Covenant into Jerusalem (see 1 Chronicles 21:26), Ezra rebuilt the altar when the Israelites returned from exile in Persia (see Ezra 3:3), Nehemiah constructed an altar when the wall of Jerusalem was rebuilt and the people sealed a new covenant to God (see Nehemiah 10:34), and Ezekiel prophesied of the new temple which would contain God's glory and an altar (see Ezekiel 43).

These are just a few examples of the importance of the altar in the journey of God's people. Amazingly, we see the altar appear again in two prominent visions of heaven where both Isaiah (see Isaiah 6:1-7) and John (see Revelation 8:1-5) describe the Throne of God. The altar is the prominent symbol of worship from ages past to the future because of its place in the story of the redemption.

The altar symbolizes worship, sacrifice, and remembrance. During the old covenant, it was a place—first a moveable tabernacle and second, a temple in Jerusalem. In the new covenant it lies within us. 1 Corinthians 6:19 says, "Do you not know that your body is a temple of the Holy Spirit

Milepost 5: *Altaring* Moments

with you, whom you have from God?" No longer do we *go* to a place to worship; worship takes place within our very being.

The aspect I want to focus on is the idea of remembrance as an act of worship. Just like the Israelites, we are also on a journey of restoration. God is in the process of restoring a relationship that was lost by sin (see 1 Peter 5:10), and transforming us into the image of his Son (see 2 Corinthians 3:18). There are supernatural, transient moments that take place in our lives along the path. The average Christian often reasons these moments away as fate or mere circumstance, but to the one who possesses the insight that wisdom provides, these moments are *altaring* moments.

Altaring moments are huge, life-changing events where God shows himself strong on our behalf (see 2 Chronicles 16:9). My proposal is for us to stop, meditate upon, and engrain these moments into our memory as an act of worship. Basically, to create an altar in our own story—a memorial marker of God's provision along our journey, just like the Israelites did. This is important because the Christian life is not about starting strong; it's about finishing well and persevering through the trials, tribulations, and circumstances of life. Without these markers in our lives, we become susceptible to doubt, depression, and worry.

Remember, Satan always comes to steal, kill, and destroy what is ours in Christ (see John 10:10). On the other hand, an individual that practices remembrance has an ability to recall the past provision of God. This builds and encourages faith, hope, and peace. My concern is that if we forget the steps of redemption and transformation in our lives, we will forget the meaning of the journey...and ultimately disengage rather than find intimacy with God through worship.

An *Altared* Culture

From the beginning of Jesus' ministry he was accused of forgetting the former requirements of God. During the Sermon on the Mount he began to describe what the Kingdom of God looked like. In other words he was painting a picture of this proposed culture of worship. Some accused him of being a radical zealot, trying to blaspheme and destroy what God had previously established. In response he stated, "Do not think that I have come to abolish the Law and Prophets; I have not come to abolish them but to fulfill them" (Matthew 5:17).

Jesus' purpose was not to forget the former but to memorialize God's law and story of redemption so that he could create a culture that fulfilled God's purpose. In essence Jesus was creating a culture that acknowledged and remembered God in every aspect of their lives. This is worship.

Previously, I stated that Jesus lived in the moment because he only did and said what was currently proceeding out of the mouth of God. At first glance these two ideas—spontaneously following God's voice and remembering—can seem to be a mutual contradiction. I propose that they are just the opposite...that they are perfectly matched.

Notice how many times Jesus says, "You have heard it said..." Is Jesus just making stuff up? Certainly not, he is reminding his followers of what God has said in the past. The fact that he was a rabbi meant that he had been well-educated in the Holy Words of the Old Testament. But if we look back to the last days of his ministry, we must ask the question, *Why would Jesus ask the disciples to break bread and drink wine in remembrance of him* (see Luke 22:14-23)? I believe it is because he knew they would forget.

Every person's heart is prone to wander from the path of life. Jesus knew that without a culture of *altaring* moments, it would be impossible to stay the course. Would it have been possible for Jesus to withstand temptation without remembering God faithfulness and provision? Would it have been possible for Jesus to withstand the beating and crucifixion that resulted in his death without the previous *altaring* moment in the Garden of Gethsemane?

Milepost 5: *Altaring* Moments

In that moment Jesus went to the secret place to pour his heart out to God and remember the purpose for which he had been called. He paused, stopped, and worshipped by willingly laying down his life; this enabled him to walk the difficult narrow road that lay before him. Without these *altaring* moments, the journey is too tough to traverse.

This path of restoration begins with acknowledging that salvation comes through Christ alone and that each and every step is a continual act of worship. The remembrance of God's previous acts of grace and steadfast love toward you enables you to have the faith to create a culture in which others are led to do the same!

Remembering in an *Altared* Culture

God calls us to remember the faithfulness and steadfast love he has shown. In a culture that is consumed with immediacy and the next new thing, we often look on the past with such disdain that we lose the ability extract from it all that God desires. In our zeal for what the future may hold, we ignore the steps that have gotten us to our current place.

Within the culture that I envision, remembrance has a prominent place because we have been called to make disciples (worshippers) of all the nations (see Matthew 28:19-20). This requires us to go places and do things that only the power of God dwelling within us can do (see Acts 1:8). In the establishment of the Kingdom of God, we will experience spiritual warfare, insurmountable odds, and discouraging circumstances. All of God's chosen people throughout history have faced the same battle. Those who forget what God has done in the past are the most likely to lose heart and disengage from the mission. But those who have a firm foundation of remembrance of the *altaring* moments in their lives will continue and prevail.

Worship is more encompassing than just our personal sacrifice; it requires us not only to look to the future with hope and faith, but also to hang onto every transcendent moment of the past. This allows us to have a more complete view of what God is doing in our lives. Each moment of our life is an invitation to worship by remembering what God has done!

Application

Perhaps, as you have been reading this chapter, some of those *altaring* moments have come to mind. Get out a piece of paper and write them down. They might be moments of crisis or of elation where God came through. Maybe they are painful, and you have tried to erase them from your memory. I encourage you to dig deep and recover these moments of your journey.

Remember that God is orchestrating every step along your journey with the desire for your freedom. This freedom allows each step to result in a greater resemblance of Christ in our lives. After these moments have come to mind, ask God, "What were you teaching me in this moment?" When he reveals his purpose, place a memorial marker in your mind. Stop and worship as God shows you his steadfast and consistent presence in your life. Record these moments. Place them in a timeline and be amazed at what God has done in your life.

Finally, share your story with those closest to you. There is nothing more encouraging to see than a transformed life. Your *altaring* moments will actually lead others to worship. Go lead worship with your life!

Section 4
Our Culture Destination

Chapter 12

Creating Culture

    The last eleven years of my life have been an experiment in leadership. I have devoured every available leadership book, painstakingly searching each page to find the one magic solution that would unlock my hidden potential. Leadership conferences left my mind racing with new innovations that I impatiently introduced into our church. Each conversation with a fellow worship leader left me evaluating their systems and processes, trying to figure out if they knew something that had escaped my understanding. I have spent most of my years trying to reproduce a personalized conglomeration that replicates all the knowledge I have gathered.
    And guess what? It hasn't always worked.
    I am not exactly sure of the motive behind this consuming resolve, but I know the Spirit has implanted an innocent craving that seems to be misled by my actions. I believe there is a desire that pulsates through every follower of Christ: "God, make a difference through my life." As you may imagine, I have always wanted to create a culture of worship within my church and in my city. I long for the day I can see people engage with God in the midst of every circumstance of their life. I long to see the people of God praise His name when life stinks, when pain has encompassed their soul, or when sin ravages their life and leads them to a place of utter desperation. I have always had a vision to see people who used to *curse* God be radically transformed to worship him from the same mouth.
    The vision itself was not wrong. It was God-given, God-honoring, and pure. It was the method I was using to achieve

the vision that needed attention. I was trying to create a culture based upon my own leadership ability and personal strength, which as many of you know, ultimately ends in failure.

Henry Blackaby states, "God isn't looking for proven leaders; He's looking for those who have hearts that are pure and responsive, and then He equips them by His Spirit to be leaders. The Lord is looking not for the talented, but for the obedient. He's looking not for the skilled, but for those who are sensitive to His Spirit."[xxxii] Before we delve into how to actually create an *altared* culture of worship through the power of the Holy Spirit, let's first reflect on another hero of our faith that made the same mistake.

Watch me "Let My People Go"

Moses, the son of a Hebrew slave, was miraculously saved by the hand of God when his tethered, tar-covered basket was discovered by royalty. Moses was found by none other than the daughter of Pharaoh, king of Egypt. Moses was educated in the highest knowledge in the known world at that time, raised in a palace, and honored as a member of the sovereign ruling family. If anybody could create a new culture, he could.

Moses possessed the power, the skill, and the raw desire that should have enabled him to lead powerfully and effectively in the world. It just so happens that young Moses tried his hand at changing culture in his own strength. Scripture says, "When he was grown up, [he] refused to be called the son of Pharaoh's daughter, choosing rather to be mistreated with the people of God than to enjoy the fleeting pleasures of sin. He considered the reproach of Christ greater wealth than the treasures of Egypt, for he was looking to the reward (Hebrews 11:24-26).

If there were ever a noble cause, this would certainly qualify. Moses saw the inhuman slavery of his people and

Creating Culture

wanted to free them from their oppression. Let's explore further to see Moses' first step toward liberation.

> "One day when Moses had grown up, he went out to his people and looked on their burdens, and he saw an Egyptian beating a Hebrew, one of his people. He looked this way and that, and seeing no one; he struck down the Egyptian and hid him in the sand. When he went out the next day, behold, two Hebrews were struggling together. And he said to the man in the wrong, "Why do you strike your companion?" He answered, "Who made you a prince and a judge over us? Do you mean to kill me as you killed the Egyptian?" Then Moses was afraid, and thought, "Surely the thing is known." When Pharaoh heard of it, he sought to kill Moses. But Moses fled from Pharaoh and stayed in the land of Midian." (Exodus 2:11-15)

Can you imagine the abandonment that Moses must have felt as he fled for his life, a disillusionment which ultimately left him wandering through the deserts of Midian? I imagine his conversation with God sounding something like this... "God, I thought you had placed that desire within me. Was it wrong to be bold and take the cause into my own hands? I thought they would love me for my fierce resolve to free them. Yet they rejected me and mocked me. Do they not know my sacrifice?" I believe this experience left Moses dumbfounded, reeling in a cloud of confusion, because he thought he was strong enough and smart enough to accomplish the mission.

Moses failed because he acted prematurely and out of his own strength. He was zealous for God and his people, but before he could ever change a culture or create a culture, he had to be obedient and responsive to God rather than to his own desire. He had to look outside himself for the answer.

Our Culture Destination

Following in the Footsteps

Modern-day Christians often find themselves in this same place. We so easily follow the lead of Moses, which in due course leaves us confused and estranged from God's mission for our lives. Ministry in our own strength lacks the supernatural power and love of God that our churches and surrounding culture so desperately need. In this last section of the book I will describe the destination of this newly proposed culture.

Like he did with Moses, God will eventually allow us to fail, not for our destruction, but to teach us humility. The vision that He wants to reveal through the Spirit is important enough to allow you to fail. Often our own personal failure brings us to a place where we can *dependently* lead through the power of his Spirit rather than *independently* trusting our own ability. Creating a culture was God's idea from the beginning. Let's look at how it all began.

He Spoke, We Speak

The creative side of God's character has been present from the beginning of time. After all, we refer to him as the "Creator" because he is the one who creates! One of the unique qualities of God is that he creates out of nothing. The manner in which he does this is fantastically mysterious and beyond our understanding: He *spoke* all that we know into existence.

The psalmist says, "For, he spoke, and it came to be; he commanded, and it stood firm" (Psalm 33:9). In Genesis chapter 1 alone, the statement "God said" occurs ten times. Not only did God create the universe, but he also uniquely crafted the relational web between Himself and all humanity...which we refer to as "culture."

God first initiated the idea of culture when He made Adam. After he saw that man needed a companion, he created a woman out of Adam's rib (see Genesis 2:21-22). Genesis

Creating Culture

1:27 states, "So God created man in his own image, in the image of God he created him; male and female he created them." For the first time we see human interaction taking place between a man and a woman, but most importantly, both are in relationship with God. The relationship must have been familiar and comfortable, as evidenced by God walking and talking with them in the Garden (see Genesis 3:8).

Before we go any further, let's go back to a Scripture stated earlier: "God created man in his own image." It is important to understand that Adam and Eve were *created* in the divine image of the One who *created* them. I am not suggesting that people *are* God because God tells us, "For as the heavens are higher than the earth, so are my ways higher than your ways and my thoughts than your thoughts" (Isaiah 55:9). God created a reflection of himself, but did not recreate himself. A reflection is a picture of an original. It looks similar, operates in a similar manner, and its primary purpose is to reflect the image the original or in this case the originator.

So, if God is a creator, it should not be too much of a stretch to conclude that we are also able to create! Further along in the story we see Adam replicating exactly what his Creator had modeled. "So out of the ground the Lord God formed every beast of the field and every bird of the heavens and brought them to the man to see what he would call them. And whatever the man called every living creature that was its name" (Genesis 2:19).

Do you see the correlation? Adam is speaking the names of the animals into existence just as God spoke him into existence. Adam created because he is made in the image of the one who creates.

Not only did Adam possess the ability to create through speech, he also possessed the ability to make things with his hands. In Genesis 3:7 we see that Adam had the ability to sew fig leaves together as the first pieces of clothing. Now the context is obviously not the best because he had just committed the first sin, but even in his sin he still possessed the ability to create something new with his hands.

Scripture tells us that God created with his "hands." Psalm 8:3 states, "I look at your heavens, the work of your fingers, the moon and the stars, which you have set in place." The Psalmist goes on to ask, "What is man that you are mindful of him, and the son of man that you care for him? Yet you have made him a little lower than the heavenly beings and crowned him with glory and honor. You have given him dominion over the works of your hands; you have put all things under his feet" (Psalm 8:4-6).

God enabled man and woman to use speech and their hands to rule over the earth, just as he has created us and rules over us. It's utterly amazing and quite a task if you think about it! Let's look at what God has called us to create.

Worship: An *Altared* Culture

Let me first say that there are many different things God has called us to create, but my focus will be on what I believe is essential to our mission of making Christ followers: creating culture. "Culture" is a very complex word that has variety of meanings.

Christian cultural critic Ken Meyers identifies culture as what we make of the world.[xxxiii] Andy Crouch, author of <u>Culture Making</u>, states, "Culture is, first of all, the name for our relentless, restless human effort to take the world as it's given to us and make something else."[xxxiv] The term itself has a tendency to be rather vague, but for simplicity and clarity I will define culture by its components. Culture is enveloped in time, location, community, uniqueness, and a method of communication.

So, what are we trying to make or, should I say, create? I believe we are called to not create a generic "culture," but one that has worship at its epicenter. Jesus gave us the commission to "make disciples of all nations, baptizing them in the name of the Father and the Son and of the Holy Spirit, teaching them to observe all that I have commanded you" (Matthew 28:19). In essence, God is calling us to train people all over the world to be worshipers, followers who replicate Jesus' example of a life of worship unto His Father.

When we look at Jesus' example, we see the perfect example of worship. His life of worship points us to the Old Testament altar. The altar was a place of worship, remembrance, and acknowledgement of God holiness. Jesus lived a life that *"altered"* his culture because he led others to worship, consider, and recognize his Father. Our lives are supposed to point others to the same destination, but we often fall short of our mission.

Humanity's inclination since the fall has always been and will always be to worship itself and the tangible objects of God's creation (see Romans 1:21). Therefore, God has made it our mission to bring the gift of redemption to the world through communicating God's original intent and demonstrating the restoration of what has been lost. Unfortunately, through our zeal for change, Christians have frequently taken this mission and tried to bring about transformation through ineffective postures.

Gestures toward Culture

Andy Crouch, the editorial director for *The Christian Vision Project,* identifies and evaluates four typical responses—or "gestures"—of Christians that fall flat in their effect on the world around us.

> "The problem is not with any of these gestures – condemning, critiquing, consuming, copying. All of them can be appropriate responses to particular cultural goods. Indeed, each of them may be the only appropriate response to a particular cultural good. But the problem

comes when these gestures become too familiar, become the only way we know how to respond to culture, become etched into our unconscious stance toward the world and become postures."[xxxv]

When we constantly condemn culture, we leave no hope for redemption and lose our own voice: The world does not respond well to our negativity. If we constantly critique culture, we render ourselves ultimately reactive because we are left anxiously awaiting the next cultural thought or good to have something to discuss. An over-exposure to consuming the culture of the world will ultimately render us ineffective and disengage us from our relationship with God...because the things of the world are in opposition to God.

Finally, "When copying becomes our posture, a whole host of unwanted consequences follows. We become passive, waiting to see what interesting cultural good will be served up next for our imitation and appropriation. In fast-changing cultural domains those whose posture is imitation will find themselves constantly slightly behind the times."[xxxvi]

We often hear Christians speak of changing and transforming the "culture." Now, I do not argue that this is a noble and good ambition, but it is just not possible and ultimately not what God has called us to. Before you write me off as a heretic, please open your mind to what I believe is God's challenge to us.

Its foundation lies in a thought we discussed earlier: We are created in the image of God, thus we have the ability to create. The solution to a flawed culture is not to respond with the ineffective postures above; it is to create a redeemed culture. God has not called us to change or transform the world's culture; instead, we are to reflect and represent Him by creating something new out of the very essence of our being.

"My concern is that the modern church has become very good at replicating the world's culture, which has left them incapable of genuine creative participation in the ongoing drama of God's culture. It is dangerously detached from a God who is anything but predictable and safe."[xxxvii]

The Relevant Church

Many churches are on a search to be relevant in their culture in which they find themselves immersed. Although this is a good quest, it doesn't always lead to the right destination…unless the proper path is taken. Young Christians like to search the cultural landscape for the next new idea they can introduce to the church. Every corporate marketing slogan has the potential of being nabbed and modified to present the message of Christ.

We read relevant magazines and boast that our services are relevant because our music, sound, and lights replicate the world around us. It is true: Relevance has become a buzz word throughout Christianity. But changing the church to raise a false facade of "relevance" will never change the world! Only the life and love of Christ can change the world.

Relevance must not be our focal point. Relevance is merely the byproduct of Christians creating a genuine culture of worship. In other words, it is a natural occurrence. As we replicate the Creator by creating, we produce something that is engaging to our culture and that attracts them to an alternate way of living.

Every time we take a slogan and reshape it or write new lyrics for a song of our culture, the world around us laughs because they can easily boast "Been there, done that." It's time for the church to rise up and present something of real value, of real change and challenge to our culture instead of being passive and weak. Let's stop copying and calling it "relevant." Let's start creating a culture of worship that truly engages and introduces something our culture has never before experienced.

Cultural Components

So, what could we possibly create that could have this level of impact? We must start with the basic components of every culture: time, location, community, uniqueness, and a method of communication. The time is now, your generation, your lifetime. The location is wherever you are at the moment. The community is your family, office, neighborhood, church, and city. Uniqueness simply implies that you are going to offer something to the world that they have never experienced before. Finally, how are you going to communicate among the other cultural creators [those who join the mission to create an *altared* culture], and what method will you use to share it with the world.

Jesus followed this model when he commenced creating a culture that would radically impact the world. His time was when he turned 30 years old. He had three years to effectively create and implement an alternative culture. His location was the surrounding towns of Judea and Samaria. His community was the outcast and rejected that no one thought were worthy of attention. He started with a small group of twelve men, came to rescue the children of Israel, challenged the religious elite, and ultimately sought to impact the estranged Gentiles.

Jesus' uniqueness was groundbreaking in that he connected people to God and preached the kingdom of God through personal sacrifice, not military control. In his own passionate pursuit to do and say what his father was doing and saying, his method of communication was parables and miraculous signs. Through the use of these culture components, he established and invited others to live within a culture that honored His Father and led others to do the same.

We now create culture in the same way. Notice how I have used personal stories throughout this book that have

Creating Culture

explained my journey to create an *altared* culture of worship. Just like me, you also have a story of redemption in your life. Your stories paint beautiful masterpieces that make truths visible to the imagination of the hearer's heart. They point others toward the path that Jesus walked: the path to intimacy. In other words they display a visible representation of what it means to do and say what God is doing. Finally, we only do this through the strength and power that has been deposited in us by the Holy Spirit. Only by him are we able to see the miraculous tangibly in our lives.

So what might an *altared* culture look like in your church and context? I do not believe that culture is restricted solely to the contents of this book. This is merely a summary to date of what God has shown me on the subject. I am sure that throughout the years I will have many more chapters to write about God's heart for worship.

It quite possible that you have thought of aspects that could be included too; that is the beauty of community. From the beginning, both culture and worship were never meant to be experienced alone—they have always been a corporate act, combining all that God has done individually in the lives of other believers.

Although I do not know the intricacies of the culture that you will create, I know that it will contain *altaring* moments. The culture must embrace acts of remembrance as well as worship because both aspects are essential to create and sustain a culture. A culture that only begins well has little impact, but one that is centered upon worshipping God and is reinforced by *altaring* moments on the journey has a significantly higher chance of succeeding in its purpose.

A Note on Music

In the context of all we have discussed about culture-building, one could easily ask, "What role does music play in this culture?" Good question! I believe music plays a vital role in teaching the body of Christ. Psalm 149:1 says, "Praise the Lord! Sing to the Lord a new song, his praise in the assembly of the godly!" Scripture is clear that we are to gather and sing songs of worship and adoration to our Lord (Ephesians 5:19-21). And the purpose of this is to reinforce our desperation for God, as well as remind us of God's steadfast, faithful character throughout the story of redemption in our lives.

In the midst of a service, we see people connecting with God in every circumstance of life. One person has just lost a job, another has received a promotion, one feels distant from God, another embraces the immersion and power of the Spirit in their lives. During times of corporate worship we encourage one another and encounter God (see Hebrews 10:23-25); we open our hearts to allow the Spirit of God to search the depths of our heart (see Psalm 139:23-24). When we have heard from the Word of Christ, our faith increased. That is when we gain the ability to go out and replicate this same atmosphere (culture) of unity and worship in our surrounding society.

Your Strength? His Strength?

It might be easy for some of you reading this book to say, "I am not comfortable creating culture; that is not my personality." It is true that some people are more suited to communicate than others, but the responsibility does not solely rest upon their shoulders. Henry Blackaby admits,

> "It is so much easier to simply do whatever we're good at than it is to walk with God and obey Him when He asks us to do what we're unable to do in our own strength. That kind of obedience requires a relationship that's close enough to identify His will, a faith that's strong enough to trust His will, and a heart that's humble enough to submit to His will. So if you intend to serve Him only according to your

Creating Culture

aptitudes and desires, you'll miss most of what He wants to do in your life."xxxviii

In other words it is far easier to copy the world and remain safely passive than to allow the Spirit of God to give you his creativity to introduce things new and innovative...and to trust in his power rather than your own abilities to implement it. Are you willing to venture into the landscape of uncertainty to fashion something new?

The Flaming Shrub

Remember our hero at the beginning of the story? Moses stepped out in his own strength and utterly failed. He lost everything and spent half his life wandering through the desert following a herd of sheep. It wasn't until God met Moses in a flaming shrub—in a secret and undisclosed place—that his life changed. And surprisingly, God affirmed Moses' original mission.

God had also heard the cries of his people and seen their affliction. He too longed to bring them out of slavery so he could renew a worship culture among them. But this time was different! Moses knew he could not accomplish such a task in himself...and this was right where God wanted him. No longer would Moses dare claim he had any strength left within himself to accomplish such a mission.

It is at this time that God reveals himself as *I AM WHO I AM*: "Say to the people of Israel, 'I am has sent me to you'" (Exodus 3:14). From that point on, Moses changed the course of history. But it was only because God provided the strength and ability to manifest Moses' vision. Moses had to follow a herd of sheep for forty years before God was willing to use him to lead.

Jesus followed a similar path and led from the place of serving God and serving others. In order to create a culture that has lasting influence, you must first be a servant. Then and only then will God release you to lead and create an *altared* culture of worship.

Application

As you read through this chapter, I imagine that many emotions and thoughts about creating were evoked. It is possible that the Holy Spirit is awakening some deep passions that were dormant way down in your soul. I urge you to not just dismiss them as impossible thoughts but to excavate those deeply-rooted visions.

If you are experiencing some new, radical ways of communication that could lead others toward an *altared* culture, offer those ideas to God and to others who can hear God on your behalf. Remember, do not repeat Moses' mistake and engage your mission prematurely from your own ability.

Finally, if you are like me, you may need to repent for many of your life endeavors. Most of us have unknowingly trusted in our own strength or simply been disengaged in God's greater purposes for our lives. Ask God to awaken in you a passion to create and not copy, to replicate instead of repress what he himself has placed within you. Surrender, embrace, and create!

Chapter 13

Leading Tribal Worship

Every week we get together to discuss what has taken place in our lives throughout that week. It happens in a variety of places...in the back yard, friend's houses, grocery stories, through emails, phone calls, and especially when we all gather to worship. The conversation is usually based upon what God is doing in our lives and what he has specifically revealed to us that week that has lead us to worship.

When we are distraught, we remind each other what God has previously done and celebrate the excitement of something new that has been revealed. The most exciting topic of our conversation is how we have created a culture that has led others to join in our conversation. It happens almost every week: A person shares how God used them to positively affect another person's life. What could be more exciting than seeing people led to worship?

What am I describing? you might ask. It's a tribe! A tribe of individuals whose mission is to create an *altared* culture of worship. Come on, take the next step on the path and see what is just around the bend. The tribe is waiting!

What's a Tribe?

Throughout this book we have described the path that leads toward a culture of worship. For those of you who are more practically-minded, you might be asking, "How are these concepts fleshed out in real life?" Well, in a word, Tribe. A worship tribe to be exact. I am inviting you to lead, build, and participate in tribal worship.

Our Culture Destination

Now I know your mind is already scrolling through your hard-drive of memories and associations with the term "tribe." What comes to mind? Do you see ancient Native Americans dressed in ceremonial regalia, participating in a rain dance around a bonfire? Or do you imagine a forgotten primitive culture deep within the jungle, unnoticed and untouched by the modern world? Does your mind run first to a modern conceptualization or the last episode of *Survivor*?

While each of these illustrations could be justified as an example of a tribe, I want to expand your mind and vocabulary to apply this term to our proposed culture of worship. Seth Godin defines a tribe in this manner, "A tribe is a group of people connected to one another, connected to a leader, and connected to an idea."[xxxix] If you define it this way, a tribe represents something familiar to us all: a group.

The word itself, however, evokes something in us even more primal to our core. That "something" is a clear mission that is enveloped around a group of people. The tribe does not include the occasional church attendee or those who sit passively on the sidelines. It doesn't include those who are ambivalent concerning the mission of Christ. The term *tribe* calls its participants to action!

So, what is that action? The members of the tribe will build an *altared* worship culture in every context of their own lives and then lead others to do the same. Some of you may be thinking, "Hold on now. I understand my identity as a creator and worshipper, but I am uncomfortable with leading anything." You are perfectly normal for having such a thought, but it is my purpose in this chapter to solidify that every person—no matter their personality—either lives to draw people closer to Christ or to passively ignore him.

Second, I want to activate in you a deep-rooted passion to lead others into worship. I know this lies within your core because the Holy Spirit lives in you. Remember, you are created in God's image: You have the mind of Christ, and you are being transformed to His likeness. If this is true, then you will have the same desires that Christ possessed. As these desires flow through you, they will be contagious to those around you.

Jesus left us with these potent words, "I tell you the truth, anyone who has faith in me will do what I have been doing. He will do even greater things than these, because I am going to the Father. And I will do whatever you ask in my name, so that the Son may bring glory to the Father. You may ask me for anything in my name, and I will do it" (John 14:12-14 NIV). Jesus came to create and guide a tribe of worshipers that would draw the whole world to acknowledge and reverence his Father; we now share that mission. He has promised us empowerment when we follow his mission.

You Want Me to Lead?

Many who know themselves to be Christ-followers experience fear and uncertainty when confronted with the term, "Leadership." After all, they responded to Jesus' call, "Follow me," not "Lead me," correct? The thought of confidently rallying people and communicating vision and mission seems foreign to those who don't think of themselves in those terms. On the other hand, those who recognize God's calling to lead, eagerly and often impatiently embrace the task at hand.

Now, the simple conclusion we might draw from past experience would be to let the leaders lead and the followers follow, but I would like to propose another approach to leadership revolving around a team. Let's explore the ramifications of that thought by looking at the many facets of leadership in an *altared* culture.

If you were to ask any member of the worship teams I lead to define my philosophy of leadership, they would tell you it's based upon a team approach. I constantly define and reiterate their identity as worship leaders. The person who plays drums in the back corner is just as important as the person leading the congregation in song. We are collectively leading the body of Christ together. If one member of the team is disengaged from leading people to worship God, then not only does the team suffer, but the congregation as a whole misses an important component. The missing component is unity.

Paul encouraged the church at Ephesus to lead in unity when he wrote, "I urge you to live a life worthy of the calling you have received. Be completely humble and gentle; be patient, bearing with one another in love. Make every effort to keep the unity of the Spirit through the bond of peace" (Ephesians 4:1-3 NIV). From Paul's instruction I would emphasize two important ideas. First, it is difficult to keep unity in leadership. Notice that he instructs them to "make every effort" which means work is involved. Unity is not natural; it cannot be derived from human strength. It is a byproduct of living a life cognizant of the Spirit of God in each person.

The second component is that unity and the Spirit of God are interconnected. Unity is the essence of the Holy Spirit because he lives in perfect unity with the Father and the Son. Thus, when the Spirit of God inhabits our individual bodies, he empowers us to live in unity with those surrounding us who have been sealed with the same Spirit (see Ephesians 1:13).

Have you ever experienced a transcendent moment where you felt the bond of peace and unity within a personal relationship, around a dinner table with your family, or in a corporate worship service? The secret components that make this possible are the presence of the Holy Spirit and the unity of purpose and passion in your group.

If we want to experience the presence of God in our leadership as we create a culture of worship, there must be an emphasis on love for one another (see 1 John 3:18-19). If we are not able to love those who are tangibly surrounding us, how will we ever represent God to our society? We must lead collectively with unity if we are to correctly build an authentic culture of worship.

Interconnection

When we talk about creating culture, we are obviously referring to one in which worship is its focal point, but I am reminded of another culture from my experience where unity was also the critical factor.

During my younger days, as stated earlier in the book, I had a passion for playing baseball. During my senior year of high school we had ample supply of talent, but as the season began, we quickly realized that we lacked unity. Every athlete was playing the game under his own agenda at the forefront of his mind. As a result, we had effectively solidified a culture of losing! Remember, you can't change a culture; the only solution is to create a new one.

Mid-season we decided to create a culture of winning, but it meant that we would have to find a way to achieve unity as a team. After trying many different processes and systems, we achieved our goal and became 4A North Carolina state champions.

Although a baseball team accomplishes its mission as a team, each individual plays a separate and equally important role. There is a definite leader who is known as a coach, and the players are all interconnected. A coach without a team is useless, just as a pitcher can't function without a catcher. It is impossible to create a winning culture without interconnectedness...which is built on a foundation of unity.

Although a unified, winning baseball team makes for a good experience, what we are reaching for in a worship team means a whole lot more. But the skills are similar. You build a tribe that leads people into worship using a similar paradigm. There is a definite leader of the tribe, but each person plays a unique and specialized role in the group. Paul referred to this interconnected relational web when he described the church as a body.

> "For the body does not consist of one member but of many. If the foot should say, "Because I am not an eye, I do not belong o the body," that would not make it any less a part of the body. If the whole body were an eye, where would be the sense of hearing? If the whole body were an ear, where would be the sense of smell? But as it is, God arranged the members in the body, each one of them, as he chose. If all were a single member, where would the body be? As it is, there are many parts, yet one body. That there may be no division in the body, but that the members may have the same care for one another" (1 Corinthians 12:14-20,25)

Without this interconnected unity, it is impossible to create a worship tribe that can build culture and *altar* our society. Before we discuss the definition and parameters of that worship culture, let's look at the individual component of leadership within a tribe.

Individual Leadership

A tribe is not only a collective force, it is also made up of individuals. It is important to note that a tribe is only as strong as its individual members. C. J. Mahaney says, "The single greatest contribution you can make to a group is your own passionate pursuit of God."[xl] In the worship context this means that each individual has to become a worship leader to positively affect the tribe. What do I mean by that? Am I telling you to dust off that guitar buried in the abyss of your closet, practice a few weeks, and then head to work to lead some songs during lunch break? Probably not!

Let's go back to the issue of identity. Nearly every week I remind our worship leaders that they are just as much a leader of worship in their home, work place, and grocery store as they are on the stage. Respected worship leader Bob Kauflin comments in his book *Worship Matters*,

> "It doesn't matter whether we're leading a congregation, driving our car, or sitting alone in our bedroom. Everything we do should be governed by one goal – to see Jesus Christ praised, exalted, magnified, lifted up, and obeyed. Every time we open our mouths, we're leading others. A leader's spiritual life is never a private matter. If the way we live doesn't back up what we proclaim on Sunday morning, we're not only deceiving the church – we're misrepresenting the God we claim to be worshiping."[xli]

What I am stating is simply this… You have the ability to affect the environment around you. Every person communicates and exudes something from their being. It's not just with our words and the rules we follow. Being worship leaders is far more about who you are than what you do. The way you interact with those around you either leads them toward Christ (which is what a worship leader does) or toward a false illusion or substitution for God.

The problem is that most people are ignorant of their calling to lead others to worship God. Why would God make us in his image, a reflection of himself, and transform us toward the image of his Son if he did not want us to lead others to worship him?

Paul comments on this subject, "Thanks be to God, who always leads us in triumphal procession in Christ and through us spreads everywhere the fragrance of the knowledge of him. For we are to God the aroma of Christ among those who are being saved and those who are perishing" (2 Corinthians 2:14-15).

Communication

One component that is necessary for any tribe to function correctly is clear communication. "A group needs only two things to be a tribe: a shared interest and a way to communicate."[xlii] Not only does it need appropriate methods for communication within itself, it must also be able to effectively communicate its mission to the surrounding public. So before we talk about mission, let's first discuss how the tribe can communicate.

First, worshipers who want to participate in this tribe must vocalize their commitment to lead others to worship. This can be done in a variety of ways, through personal conversations, blog posts, Facebook, Twitter, or a variety of other social networking tools. The most common way of communicating is through worshiping together in unity in the local church. In this environment people who belong to this tribe can become aware of others who are also interested in living a life of worship.

What is the context of the conversation? It's simple. It mainly revolves around how we create an *altared* culture in every aspect of our lives. For example, I often ask, "How can I lead my wife to love God more?" When I go to buy groceries, I ask, "How can I create a culture of worship as I shop?" When I come up with ideas, I simply share them with those around me who desire to affect society.

Leader + Idea + Communication = Movement

Author Seth Godin states, "Great leaders create movements by empowering the tribe to communicate. They establish the foundation for people to make connection, as opposed to commanding people to follow them."[xliii] We have all seen it over the experiences that comprise our life's journey: a leader who feels the need to force an agenda. For too long the church (world-wide) has been forcefully imposing its message, not only upon those on the outside looking in, but also on the ones who willfully subject themselves to this negative atmosphere. My plea is that instead of trying to force society through critique and disdain to adopt the worldview we approve, let's create something they can't help but be caught up in.

"We need a passionate vision, not just a common idea."[xliv] The passionate vision has not changed. When did we stop believing that it was possible to carry out the mission Jesus so clearly gave us? When did we stop dreaming about the day when people in our family, city, state, and every nation, tribe, and tongue will worship God? Jesus did not give his life for a tribe who would just camp out in a begrudging mire of mediocrity; Jesus' tribe are those who passionately invest their souls in a movement that creates a culture of worship.

For a worship tribe, passion and unity with a clear vision are at its core. "For tribes, average can mean mediocre. Not worth seeking out. Boring."[xlv] So, my question to you is, "Are you satisfied with the status quo? Are you content with worshipping God for one hour a week and then wandering without any real meaning, purpose, and power through the other 99% of your week?" Don't waste the time you have spent reading this book! Start now by creating the worship culture throughout your life.

Here is the truth in the society in which we live: Average products and mediocre ideas are quickly forgotten. I am not suggesting that the mission of the Church or the sacrificial death and resurrection of Jesus has somehow lost it relevancy. Without that sacrifice, none of this would be possible. What I am challenging is *how* the church communicates and embodies the mission of Christ. God has uniquely designed you, given pastors to equip you, and empowered you with gifts and talents for the purpose of creating a culture of worship. So create.

Will You Take the Lead?

I am inviting you into a movement. Not only that, I am asking you to help lead a movement through your worship tribe and your own life individually to help others encounter God's forgiveness and purpose for their lives. Is it in you? You lead both through being interconnected with the tribe and individually as you interact with those around you.

"Leadership comes when your hope and optimism are matched by a vision of the future and a way to get there. People won't follow you if they don't believe you can get to where you say you are going."[xlvi] Are you experiencing God every day? Does eternal life with God start now? Do you know how to worship God in every season and step of the journey? If so, teach others to do the same.

"When you lead without compensation, when you sacrifice without guarantees, when you take risk because you believe, then you are demonstrating your faith in the tribe and its mission."[xlvii] Do you really believe it is possible to create a culture of worship? Will you give your life to that great cause?

Everything is On the Line

George Barna in his book *The Seven Faith Tribes* states, "The future of America is at stake, that future can best be advanced by the efforts of our faith tribes."[xlviii] It is true… Everything is on the line, and the one person God has placed upon the Earth for this situation is you. Now is the time to create; today is the day of worship!

The world is starving to find meaning in this life, and every society that lacks the worship of God at its epicenter has been weighed and found wanting. Godin exhorts his readers to action when he writes, "I don't think we have any choice. I

Leading Tribal Worship

think we have an obligation to change the rules, to raise the bar, to play a different game, and to play it better than anyone has any right to believe is possible."[xlix] I agree wholeheartedly, the commission of Jesus Christ to go and make Christ followers everywhere is the most important thing in which we will participate. Let's give our lives to create something new and do it better than anyone thought was possible. Christ followers are at their core worshipers of God. Today, every person you come in contact with—their soul is in the balance. Will you passively sit on the sidelines, mimic our society, and call it relevant? Or will you proactively create an *altared* culture of worship in your tribe and change people's perception of Jesus for eternity? God created you for such a time as this. Go create, worship, and influence the world through your worship!

About The Author

Eric Freeman has a passion to help people encounter and walk with God in every context of their lives. He primarily does this through the tool and expression of music, but also teaches what resonates in the core of his being through writing. He is based out of Greensboro, NC and spends a majority of his time raising up future worship leaders and creating culture within his local church, Daystar Church. He has a strong desire to lead current and future generations into an authentic encounter with God through music, teaching, and relationship. His partner in this journey is his lovely wife Amanda.

Acknowledgements

It is certain that all the ideas presented in the book are not original, but come from a host of research, personal experience, and most importantly relationships within my life. I must first thank my mentor, Ross Parsley, without whom this book may never have come to fruition. Ross' encouragement, inspiration, and challenges gave me the confidence I needed to pursue this dream. Personal friend and Editor Jerome Daley also deserves a large amount of recognition for his long hours of dedication, belief, and refinement of this manuscript. I would like to also acknowledge my pastor, Allen Holmes, who taught me my identity as a worshiper while providing ample opportunity for me to flourish and grow as a leader.

A special thanks, honor, and respect to my parents for raising me within a home that honored Christ and still to this day they model the life of a worshipper who can worship in any context. Meredith Tanner, Chelsea Johnson and Trevor Brock, my personal friends and Daystar partners, gave a large amount of time focused on editing and publishing to help this book effectively communicate the intended message. Jared Anderson, a fellow song writer and worship leader, has given me much inspiration, and challenged me to voice the passions within my soul. Thanks for listening. Thanks to author and friend Glenn Packiam for your belief in my ability, and building the faith in me that God would bring my project to the public. Finally, my loving, beautiful, and selfless Amanda has allowed me to spend many hours away as I have learned to be an author. She respectfully listened and read each line many times in an attempt to help me communicate my heart. Thank you for your love, support, and steadfast resolve to walk this journey with me.

NOTES

Chapter 1 – The Uncharted Journey

[i] This idea drawn from Andy Crouch, *Culture Making: Recovering Our Creative Calling*, (Downers Grove, IL. Inter Varsity Press, 2008), 43, 44.

[ii] Crouch, 23.

Chapter 3 – Water, Water, Everywhere...But Not a Drop to Drink

[iii] John Piper, *A Hunger for God: Desiring God Through Fasting and Prayer*, (Wheaton, IL: Crossway Books, 1997), 60.

Chapter 4 - It's the Beginning of Wisdom

[iv] Goodrick, W. Edward & Kohlenberger R. John III. *Strongest NIV Concordance*, (Grand Rapids, MI: Zondervan, 1999), 1419.

[v] John Bevere, *The Fear of the Lord: Discover the Key to Intimately Knowing God*, (Lake Mary, FL: Charisma House, 2006), 72.

[vi] Goodrick, W. Edward & Kohlenberger R. John III. *Strongest NIV Concordance*, (Grand Rapids, MI: Zondervan, 1999), 1539.

[vii] Bevere, 122-123.

viii David Peterson, *Engaging with God: A Biblical Theology of Worship*, (Downers Grove, IL: InterVarsity Press, 1992), 283.

ix Bevere, 176.

Chapter 5 – The Path to Intimacy

x Goodrick, W. Edward & Kohlenberger R. John III. *Strongest NIV Concordance*, (Grand Rapids, MI: Zondervan, 1999), 1456

xi Ibid., 1575.

xii Ibid., 1580.

xiii Watchman Nee, *The Release of The Spirit*, (New York, NY: Christian Fellowship Publishers, Inc., 2000), 12.

xiv Ibid., 17-18.

xv Ibid., 25.

xvi Watchman Nee, *The Normal Christian Life*, (Carol Stream, IL: Tyndale House Publishers, Inc., 1957), 187.

xvii Ibid., 14-15.

Chapter 8 – Mile Post 2: The Anchor of Identity

xviii Nee, *The Normal Christian Life*, 102.

xix Ibid., 158.

Chapter 9 – Mile Post 3: Childhood Fantasies

[xx] PRINCE CASPIAN by C.S. Lewis copyright © C.S. Lewis Pte. Ltd. 1951. Extract reprinted by permission, 139-140.

[xxi] Ibid., 147.

[xxii] Ibid., 149.

[xxiii] Ibid., 153-154.

[xxiv] Bevere, 123.

Chapter 10 – Mile Post 4: Choose What is Best

[xxv] Joanna Weaver, *Having a Mary Heart in a Martha World: Finding Intimacy with God in the Busyness of Life*. (Colorado Springs, CO: Water Brook Press, 2000), 100.

[xxvi] Ibid., 101.

[xxvii] Watchman Nee, *Sit Walk Stand*, (Carol Stream, IL: Tyndale House Publishers Inc., 1977), 4.

[xxviii] Taken from (*The Expository Bible Commentary, Volume 2*) by Frank E. Gaebelein. Copyright © *1990* by The Zondervan Corporation. Used by permission of Zondervan.

Man's place in the garden

Genesis 2:15, "The LORD God took the man and put him in the Garden of Eden to work it and take care of it."

The author had already noted that God "put" (wayyasem) man into the garden (v.8b). In v.15 he returned to this point and recounted the purpose for God's putting man there. Two important points from v.15 are in danger of being obscured by the English translations. The first is the change from v.8 In the Hebrew word for "put." Unlike v.8 where a common term for "put" is used, in v.15 the author uses a term (wayyannihehu) that he elsewhere has reserved for two special uses: God's "rest" or "safety," which he gives to man in the land (e.g., Genesis 19:16; Deuteronomy 3:20; 12:10; 25:19), and the "dedication" of something in the presence of the Lord (Exodus 16:33-34; Leviticus 16:23; Numbers 17:4; Deuteronomy 26:4, 10). Both senses of the term appear to lie behind the author's use of the word in v.15. Man was "put" into the garden where he could "rest" and be "safe," and man was "put" into the garden "in God's presence" where he could have fellowship with God (3:8).

A second point form v.15 that has often been overlooked in the English versions is the specific purpose for God's putting man in the garden. In most English versions man is "put" in the garden "to work it and take care of it" (le obdah ul somrah). Although the translation was as early as the LXX (2d cen.B.C.), there are serious objections to it. For one, the suffixed pronoun in the Hebrew text rendered "it" in English is feminine, whereas the noun "garden," which the pronoun refers to in English, is a masculine noun in

Hebrew. Only by changing the pronoun to a masculine singular, as the LXX has done, can it have the sense of the English versions, namely "to work" and "to keep." Moreover, later in this same narrative (3:23) "to work the ground" (la bod) is said to be a result of the Fall, and the narrative suggest that the author had intended such a punishment to be seen as an ironic reversal of man's original purpose. If such was the case, then "working" and "keeping" the garden would not provide a contrast to "working the ground."

In light of these objections, which cannot easily be overlooked, a more suitable translation of the Hebrew (le obdah ul somrah) would be "to worship and to obey". Man is put in the garden to worship God and to obey him. Man's life in the garden was to be characterized by worship and obedience; he was a priest, not merely a worker and keeper of the garden. Such a reading not only answers the objections raise against the traditional English translation, it also suits the larger ideas of the narrative. Throughout chapter 2 the author has consistently and consciously developed the idea of man's "likeness" to God along the same lines as the major themes of the Pentateuch as a whole, namely, the theme of worship and Sabbath rest.

[xxix] Ibid., 11.

[xxx] Mark Buchanan, *The Rest of God, Restoring Your Soul By Restoring Sabbath*, (Nashville, TN: Thomas Nelson, Inc. 2006), 188.

[xxxi] Ibid. 188.

Chapter 12 – Creating Culture

[xxxii] Henry Blackaby and Melvin Blackaby *Experiencing the Spirit: The Power of Pentecost Every Day*, (Colorado Springs, CO. Multnomah Books, 2009), 84.

[xxxiii] Ken Meyers, *All God's Children & Blue Suede Shoes: Christians and Popular Culture*, (Westchester, IL. Crossway), 1989.

[xxxiv] Crouch, 23.

[xxxv] Ibid., 92.

[xxxvi] Ibid., 93.

[xxxvii] Ibid., 94.

[xxxviii] Blackaby and Blackaby, 106.

Chapter 13 – Leading Tribal Worship

[xxxix] Seth Godin, *Tribes*, (London: Do You Zoom, Inc., 2008), 1.

[xl] C.J. Mahaney, Why Small Groups? (Gaithersburg, MD. Sovereign Grace Ministries, 1996), 35.

[xli] Bob Kauflin, *Worship Matters: Leadings Other to Encounter the Greatness of God*, (Wheaton, IL: Crossway Books, 2008), 44-45.

[xlii] Seth Godin, 1-2.

xliii Ibid., 23.

xliv Ibid., 26.

xlv Ibid., 32.

xlvi Ibid., 122.

xlvii Ibid., 84.

xlviii George Barna, *The Seven Faith Tribes: Who They Are, What They Believe, and Why They Matter,* (Brentwood, TN: George Barna ,2009),205.

xlix Seth Godin, 135.

Made in the USA
Charleston, SC
28 January 2017